selfistry

selfistry

A GUIDE TO EMBODYING
TIMELESS SPIRITUAL WISDOM

SARAH MARSHANK

gatekeeper press™
Columbus, Ohio

SELFISTRY

A Guide to Embodying Timeless Spiritual Wisdom

Published by Selfistry

Oakland, California USA

www.selfistry.com

Library of Congress Control Number: 2022934888

ISBN (paperback): 9781662924514

eISBN: 9781662924521

*This book is my pledge to humanity
that I will not forsake our future.*

for Roger...
With so much love &
appreciation for our
journies ~
Sarah
♥

DEDICATION

I dedicate this book to my mother, Bat Sheva Sheila Burk — daughter of Edith and William — my father, Eliyahu Eliot Charlip — son of Sylvia and Meyer, and my uncle, Avram Bud Charlip. My parents cultivated in me an enduring love of learning, the encouragement to sustain wonder, and the confidence to trust myself. My gratitude is immense.

TABLE OF CONTENTS

HOW TO READ
THIS BOOK

Take what resonates and leave the rest.

This is a handbook. It is not a textbook or a treatise. Its mission is to present compelling information in as concise a manner as possible. This being the case, I recommend you read through the content in its entirety and not get bogged down on sections or passages where you might trip. There's some deep material presented here in a way that I hope is digestible and comprehensible to any open mind — but words can get cumbersome. So don't let them hold you back.

Selfistry begins with this philosophical premise: The structure of the human interior is the same for every person. We all are made of Source (our essential nature), we exist as a unique Self (our individual human identity), and we each have the capacity to awaken an inner Witness (an abiding and objective self-awareness) that can help us orient ourselves within this mystifying and impermanent experience of being alive.

Building upon this premise, Selfistry defends the supposition that, when we attend to these three aspects of our humanness, we increase the likelihood of living a fulfilling and meaningful life.

My wish is that in reading this book you're able to see yourself afresh in these three Realms — Source, Witness, and Self — and feel inspired to bestow upon them your consistent care.

I've spent three decades studying and practicing in service to the creation of Selfistry. The information I share is not novel — though the structure, approach, and presentation of it is my own. Many traditions and individuals throughout history have shared their unique take on the timeless inquiries and topics explored herein. Many of which I have encountered over the years. Too many to name.

Therefore, I will not be referencing sources except where they flow with and support the narrative, having opted to streamline this manuscript so that the reader's experience can be easeful. I remain faithful to the notion that all wisdom and knowledge are universal — owned by none and expressed by many — and carry a deep and abiding respect for those who have informed and contributed to my life and my work.

If you find yourself hungry for more details on my personal journey, please consider reading my memoir.

WHY NOW

Living in a troubled time.

Humanity could use a reset.

This is understandable. Appropriate, even. Like checking a compass on a long journey. After all, sooner or later it's natural to stray off course.

Now appears to be one of those times.

With nearly eight billion people on the planet, natural resources dwindling, wealth disparity snowballing, racial injustices escalating, and climate change threatening us with extinction ... a collective reboot is probably a good idea.

Many of us recognize that the precarious times we're living in demand our serious consideration — asking us to look squarely at how we're managing the business of being human together.

Is this the best we can do?

I'm wholly captivated by this question, engaging all of myself and my days in wondering about the past, present, and future of humanity. When the Covid-19 pandemic arrived, my wondering quickened.

The prolonged disruption of daily routines sparked by a global lockdown has led many of us to reflect, not solely on our immediate concerns of work and health, but on deeper matters as well. The swiftly spreading deadly virus reminded us how vulnerable we are, how little we can control, and that death is inevitable.

It also underscored the preciousness of each moment.

This is why the pandemic is just the sort of event that has the potential to catalyze the type of reset I'm referring to, if we respond accordingly. While there have been other such moments in history — when hard choices had to be made and course corrections ensued — this one promises particularly dire consequences if we do not heed the call.

Considering even the most moderate climate change predictions, there's legitimate cause for concern over the future of our species. Given that we're likely in a planetary struggle for survival — not a local or regional one — all of humanity has the opportunity to come together in a way we have yet to be called. Either we forge a path to generating a bunch of win-wins everywhere, or we all lose. If we forsake this opportunity to challenge our present trajectory and instead continue with business as usual, our prospects don't look very promising.

This guidebook is an offering to our potential future. It lays down an approach — Selfistry — to support humans to be present for this precarious existential moment. It offers a way for individuals to cultivate a calm inner disposition and a readiness to act.

Selfistry's approach is simple. It maps out an easy and accessible path for self-reflection. When engaging in the quality and breadth of exploration I suggest, it becomes possible to recalibrate ourselves — contributing to the global reboot I'm referring to. This effort does not dismiss or replace the importance of initiating or enacting change in other areas — infrastructure, governance, or international relations, for example. It merely suggests that, if we each spend some time getting our own Self in order, the whole enterprise will be favorably impacted.

I understand that you may be familiar with personal development, spiritual growth, or self-help. You may also hold steadfast views on politics, religion, or social justice issues. This is all good.

Whether you are new to the territory of self-exploration or are a lifelong seeker, the approach presented here does not ask you to change anything about yourself. Instead, it offers a framework within which to see yourself afresh and presents a way to orient your self-knowledge towards living a life that will best serve the world in these uncertain times.

HOW SELFISTRY
CAME TO BE

The way of self-knowledge.

I spent my thirties sitting on a meditation cushion determined to bring about an inner shift that would finally make me happy.

Here's what I mean by happy.

I do *not* mean the fleeting emotion that's dependent upon ingestion of a substance, acquisition of a shiny object, or involvement with a particular person or place. When I speak of happiness, I'm referring to the sense of peace that can come with simply being alive — knowing who we are and why we're here, regardless of external circumstances.

Most people don't use the word happiness in this way.

For many, the definition is more reflective of what I *actually* wanted back when I was in my twenties and began my search. I wouldn't have said I wanted a sense of inner peace. I wanted to be happy — as in feeling good all the time. Energized. Constantly excited about my life.

That never happened.

My years on the cushion are what brought me to the clarity that happiness is best defined as an emotional state that comes and goes — just like sadness. I don't have anything against it. In fact, I quite enjoy feeling happy.

However, once I saw that happiness was unsustainable for long periods of time, it became clear that what I was really seeking was peace of mind — a deeper and enduring sense of ease and joy. I was longing to inhabit a state of being that is unshakeable by life's ever changing conditions, capable of informing my daily decisions, and useful for guiding my overall life direction.

It's fair to say that, rather than seeking a happy life, I was actually seeking a meaningful one. Realizing this was a huge relief. Finding what I was searching for, however, was not so simple. Or easy.

When I was growing up — in the sixties and seventies — how to access inner peace wasn't taught in school or discussed in my home. What constituted a good life was not mentioned beyond the subtle — and not so subtle — suggestions that an enviable life depended upon external matters such as physical appearance, social status, and financial success.

Though this ignorance about something so essential to being human plagued the entire society — with its significant and enduring consequences, our family didn't know what we were missing. We thought we *were* living a meaningful life.

This is some of what our lives looked like:

We stopped paying attention to our vital bond with the natural world and instead ate processed food and watched nature shows on TV.

We allowed an infatuation with our intellect to eclipse any other way of engaging the unknown, and we relegated religion to a cultural identity — casting aside its essential spiritual contribution to human life.

As immigrants escaping persecution, my ancestors got wholly swept up in the American dream and the western world's drive for dominance — personal, national, and global. They passed these values onto me — and to all of Gen X, Y, and Z — via a persistent injunction towards progress.

From a young age, the path to my happy life was clearly laid out for me. College. Career. Marriage. Kids. But something never felt quite right about it all. I had no idea what the root of my discomfort was or even how to talk about it. It was as if I couldn't see the whole picture — which included who I was capable of becoming and what life was really all about. A piece was missing.

This is some of how I felt:

It annoyed me that grownups said one thing and did another. I couldn't reconcile this contradiction and was uncertain of who to trust.

It troubled me that my grandmother rarely smiled and never talked about her feelings. I sensed her sadness was possibly my fault.

When my uncle died suddenly in his thirties, I felt buried by a blanket of heaviness I couldn't shake off.

I was totally confused about sex.

I had nobody with whom I could talk to about any of this. Either I was approaching the wrong people with my angst, or very few actually knew what the hell was going on.

I started to feel especially disillusioned once I went off to college and could see that it wasn't solely in my personal sphere that things were amiss. I noticed gaping holes and incongruities in the social and political structures all around me. I began to feel certain that the pathway pre-scribed for me — chasing the American dream — might actually lead not to a quality life, but likely only to more chasing.

My distress came to a head when I found myself unintentionally pregnant at the age of twenty-two.

The pregnancy was a radical wake-up call, bringing my uncertainty about everything into stark view. I was devastated by the situation and agonized over the choice I had to make. I did not feel ready to become a mother or to commit to a long term relationship with the father, and I was equally distraught by the alternative: ending a life.

I struggled to keep it together.

The hardest part was the loneliness I felt. I still had not met someone with whom I could talk deeply about all the ways I felt lost and whose counsel I could trust. I solicited advice from close friends and from my parents, but their suggestions reflected what felt like their own unresolved confusion. For example, having a child at twenty-two — while not yet married or out of college — was not in line with what my parents had hoped for me. Yet they did expect me to become a mother. Their advice was therefore tentative and noncommittal.

Among my peers, abortions were a fairly common occurance. Ending a pregnancy was viewed as no big deal — a liberating option for a sexually liberated woman. The psychological impact of the experience was never addressed. I'm not sure why I didn't consider adoption. I suspect that, on some level, that option felt untenable. Either I birthed and raised my child, or nobody did.

In the end, the choice was mine alone to make. Feeling ill-equipped, rushed, and unsupported, I made my decision.

A few years later, still impacted by the pregnancy — simultaneously relieved and heartbroken by my choice to end it — I began in earnest to search for a way out of what had spiraled into a relentless depression that included fantasies of ending my life. I knew that, in order to not give in to my despair, I'd have to find a way to make sense of everything that had happened. I couldn't pretend the abortion never occurred and pick up where I left off pre-pregnancy. I had to figure out how to want to live again. In other words, I had to *become* the person I hadn't yet met — somebody who actually knows what the hell is going on and is at peace in a mad world.

Though consumed with doubt, I made a calculated decision to trust that the answers I sought were out there. I simply needed to dedicate my life to finding them.

I then stepped into what I intended to be a one-year sabbatical — taking time off from my teaching job to focus solely on figuring out where and how to go looking for the wisdom I sought.

That year turned into more than ten.

Spending the first year living simply, quietly, and close to nature — pausing any focus on my career or a romantic relationship — was deeply therapeutic for my body and psyche. I had time to slow down and feel my grief rather than attempt to get over it. I had time to read books from beginning to end, taking notes and researching sources — rather than trying to absorb deep material by reading a chapter during my lunch hour or before bed. I was starting to feel like maybe I really could find my way. So when offered the opportunity to be financially supported and to remain on sabbatical indefinitely, I took it.

At that point, I could have chosen to continue my quest within the context of a normal life so as not to disrupt my career momentum or my prospects for available partners. I also considered leaning in the opposite direction and heading out on a pilgrimage to find a shaman or a guru in a foreign land. However, upon seeing the benefits of simply taking time to be fully present with myself and my questions, I thought it much more advantageous to settle in right where I was and devote myself to a robust curriculum of self-directed learning and rigorous practice.

I honestly didn't anticipate that I would be immersed in this phase of my journey for more than a decade. I thought another year, maybe two, would suffice.

But these things can take time.

During that decade, I studied numerous belief systems, ideologies, and philosophies. Gleaning from what I learned, I also practiced a variety of methods for transformation and spiritual realization. I strove to become what I was seeking rather than solely learn about it. So rather than merely educating myself on the various views of the meaning of life, I chose to engage in the ways and practices of the mystic. Instead of relying exclusively on scholarly perspectives, I chose to meditate on original texts from many of the world's religions, taking into consideration their historical context in order to determine for myself how well their teachings applied to my current life.

I hiked solo in the wilderness, listening to the whispers of the wind while tracking the seasons through the changing flora and fauna. I taught myself to garden and learned the language of soil and seeds. I managed to chop firewood without hurting myself and pour concrete without giant lumps. As my studies deepened, I began to design my own rituals and create ceremonies that offered a space for my heart to sing and cry. I picked up needlepoint as a creative exercise and baked bread from scratch. I opted for long hot baths to soothe my fear and despair. I spent thousands of hours in silence, contemplation, prayer, and meditation.

As my path of discovery was self-guided, it had some unanticipated — if predictable — pitfalls. For example, having a living teacher nearby to suggest a course correction in regard to any ascetic practice — yoga, pranayama, meditation, fasting — might have shortened the time I needed to yield a beneficial outcome, while also preventing potential harm. Lacking such a teacher, it probably took me longer than some to realize the benefits of my meditation practice. And a good teacher might have been able to prevent the chronic neck injury I sustained from doing shoulder stands.

However, despite the damage done to my body and mind through practicing an austerity incorrectly or enacting a method that simply didn't yield the anticipated results, the value of encountering such dead ends on my own and having to figure things out on the fly brought a quality of embodied knowledge that has proven to be highly stable and beneficial.

In the end, the upsides of being on my own proved more valuable than the downsides. I accumulated a wealth of knowledge, gained a deep respect for self-discipline, developed an ability to trust myself, and grew the willpower to stay the course no matter what.

I also found the answers I was seeking.

My discoveries ultimately led to the creation of Selfistry, which I formulated approximately ten years after ending my retreat. It took a good part of that ensuing decade to integrate myself back into the world and, from there, to weave all I had come to know into an offering that made sense and could be shared with others.

I'm fairly certain that most of us long for what I was seeking: the definition of — and the way to live — a meaningful life. I suspect it's a piece of what makes us human. I also imagine that many of us have an experience on par with what the pregnancy was for me — a wake-up call that shakes us to our core; a moment when we realize we are not living our best life and everyone we turn to for guidance disappoints. I like to believe that the entire world is experiencing one of those wake-up calls right now in this lingering pandemic.

I also suspect that when good guidance does come along there's a way in which our whole being recognizes it. It's like being reminded of something we already know — like discovering a secret that was tucked away in a pocket we hadn't checked in a long time.

If even one element of this book helps even one person find their way to remembering the secrets to living a better life, then it has served humanity well.

However, as you read on, please know ...

Selfistry does not deliver any absolute truths about the meaning or purpose of life. It merely creates the conditions for you to sort that out for yourself. Through all my years of study and practice, much to my surprise — and delight — I discovered that, when it comes to living a meaningful life, the fundamental guiding principles have not changed over time. They just tend to get buried now and then. The principles are simple and trustworthy — presented afresh here in the Three Realms of Selfistry — and accessible to all.

I've done my best to articulate timeless teachings in a way that will hopefully make sense to people born and raised in this era — offering insights well suited for the troubled times we live in and tools well adapted for the modern person who may not feel they have the time or need for such "spiritual" matters.

Let me also be clear on what else Selfistry is not.

Selfistry is not a prescription for self-improvement in the ways we see it represented across most of our media channels today.

Self-improvement as presently marketed and sold in the mainstream in the west is more akin to a fad than a movement of substance and enduring character. The industry feeds on a fixation with imagined outcomes and glorifies a persistent drive to go after unrealizable goals — always keeping the consumer coming back for more. Much of what is presented as self-care or self-help actually produces an unhealthy self-absorption, encouraging a drive for pleasure or achievement at the expense of others as well as the expense of one's own inner peace — if not explicitly, then certainly implicitly.

Though there are, of course, exceptions — and even evidence of a changing tide in certain areas — we would do well to slow down and take a closer look at what's really being promoted and who really benefits.

In contrast, and as a welcome antidote ...

The way of self-knowledge, as Selfistry views it, means becoming aware of where we've been misguided around what constitutes a meaningful life and resetting our compass in the direction that will grow us into the kind of humans we long to become — and the kind the world needs. This means taking a sober look at ourselves, successfully drawing out the innate potential in each of us, amplifying our sameness while celebrating our uniqueness, and unleashing our essential contribution to the well-being of all.

The good news is you do not have to go on retreat for ten years in order to accomplish this. I did that so you don't have to. It would suffice to consider deeply what you find written here and then carve out some dedicated time within the life you already have to put your attention on rebooting your inner operating system.

I understand that for some it may feel counterintuitive to focus on oneself when others are struggling and the world is reeling from so much uncertainty. It's true that many are in dire need and numerous local, national, and global systems are unstable or collapsing. It's also reasonable that we would attempt to fix what's obviously broken out in the world rather than address the murkier concerns of what's needing attention inside ourselves.

However, by prioritizing an earnest self-reflection, we really do become better able to manage the challenges in our personal lives, while simultaneously gaining clarity on how best to impact the greater web that we're part of. Over time a sense of ease and joy emerges and maybe the whole world is revived.

SELFISTRY
EXPLAINED

Know thyself.

One of the first teachers I discovered on my quest was Ramana Maharshi. He was an Indian saint of the early 20th century who taught that the way to a meaningful life, which he called self-realization, was through engaging in a process called self-inquiry: the continuous asking of the simple question *Who am I?*

Ramana promised that this self-inquiry practice will eventually lead practitioners to a conscious experience of the mystery that manifests as all life. Such a realization, he promised, would bring clarity on how to live a beautiful life. We can locate this mystery everywhere, he said, once we know how to look — but especially in the core of our very selves, buried beneath the roles we play.

"When you ask the question, *Who am I?*, don't settle for the first answer that comes," Ramana advised. "Take the answer as merely one expression of you, then set it aside and ask again. And again. Be on the lookout for what is present when no more answers appear."

Ramana is pointing towards what, in Selfistry, I call Source. He assures us that this Source is undeniably present in every human being and essential to our existence while also mysteriously appearing as if separate from us.

When I began asking the question *Who am I?*, I initially called forth answers such as, "I am Sarah, I am a woman, I am a teacher," and so on. However, as I kept asking, the obvious answers started to feel nebulous or approximate.

As I continued setting the answers aside, fewer of them arose and, eventually, something marvelous came forward into my awareness. The experience included an absence of any solid sense of Self, surrounded by an encounter with Source — which simultaneously felt like the stuff I'm made of, as well as that which wove the stuff into something in the first place.

Ramana insists that, as we persevere in our questioning, eventually this essential reality will become so obvious that we will marvel at how we ever missed it. When someone would ask him to say more about the qualities of that essential reality, he would remind the practitioner to focus on the question *Who am I?* rather than *What is truth?* He promised that answering the former question would surely address the latter.

When students would grapple with trying to understand the paradox of how we can simultaneously be Source and be separate from it at the same time, he would soothe the questioner with humor and love, guiding them back to the inquiry practice. The human mind cannot understand this paradox, he would say. However, the human being can comfortably dwell in it.

Some traditions might refer to Source as Spirit, Energy, The Mystery, or God.

Whereas Ramana chose to live a simple life and teach, others who have self-realized live in a variety of ways. It can be tricky to know whether a person is truly conscious of their existence as Source simply by examining how they live on the outside. It can also be difficult to make that judgment without having one's own conscious experience of Source.

One element common to all who have self-realized is that their place in the web of life, regardless of what that is, becomes self-evident and natural. There is a way in which a self-realized human walks on the planet that feels as if they know who they are and are right where they're supposed to be. It's as if, once a consciousness of Source is awakened and sustained over time, we no longer have to do anything special to find our purpose or place in the world. We only need to stop chasing after any unchecked goals we were taught to strive for and allow our relationship with — and as — Source to guide us.

While it's true that we are never disconnected from Source, it is also true that a lack of conscious awareness about this essential aspect of ourselves can be a major contributor to unseemly behaviors and confusion around what to do with our one precious life.

During my years in retreat, while steadily engaging in the self-inquiry practice Ramana suggests, I also took on radical ascetic practices, denying my personal self-expression in order to access this essential Source. In addition to a robust daily meditation and yoga regimen, I regularly refrained from eating and speaking, abstained from consuming media, and acquired no material possessions beyond the bare necessities.

I was testing the hypothesis that, if I erased my personal Self completely, Source would be all that was left — and if only Source remained, then I would finally be at peace forever.

Here's what actually happened.

Over time, my personal identity began to recede as a consequence of my practices and I was able to tap into a detached awareness — a part of me that was not interested in living my roles but had not yet felt herself as Source.

The Witness, as I call this objective awareness in Selfistry, was a profound discovery, and one that I approached curiously, yet gingerly.

Truth is, as I began to shed my various roles and enter into an unfamiliar detached state, I feared I might lose myself altogether and go insane. After all, I had a masters degree in education and considered myself a teacher, I had four siblings and knew myself as a sister, and now, in retreat, I was beginning to identify as a spiritual adept. These all felt like significant identities that I was reticent to completely jettison and bet everything on enlightenment. So I paced myself with caution, always keeping a role nearby, just in case I needed it.

This is why the emergence of an inner Witness was at once fascinating and frightening.

I welcomed the experience of identifying as the Witness because I still felt like a somebody. Somebody sane. I still had the experience of existing as *me*, but was no longer tethered to a persona or to any particular role.

Because I trusted in the process and the teachings of Ramana — especially after he came to me in a dream — I allowed this Witness to deepen and stabilize, primarily through the practices of meditation, fasting, solitude, and silence. As I refused to respond to the shoulds that my roles constantly berated me with, I eventually accessed a profound peace. I also found relief in knowing that I could choose to pick up those roles whenever I wanted — or never at all.

Over time, the Witness became the ground from which I could put my attention squarely on the realization of Source.

The discovery of the Witness alone would have been enough to reorient my life in beautiful ways, bringing me fully into the present moment, giving me perspective on the roles I had been conditioned to play, and making room for the possibility of exercising choice in the matter of which roles I actually *wanted* to play. After all, maybe there were new roles that I had yet to enact that might suit me even better than the ones I'd been given or taken on thus far. This possibility was compelling.

But it was the experience of Source that fundamentally changed my life forever.

As I continued to practice and stabilize as the Witness — keeping my roles at bay — Source came more and more into view. Eventually I was able to access a consistent experience of it. I began to immerse myself in Source's world, curious about how deep and far it went — and how far I could go into it before I might disappear completely ... secretly hoping that I would. This phase of my journey was profoundly nourishing and transformative, as if I had met my very existence in its most holy place.

But this was not the end of my quest.

Though many teachings speak to the realization of Source as the endpoint and the ultimate realization of a spiritual life, and though I imagined that, once there, I might want to die in its embrace, instead I encountered an unexpected aspiration to end my sabbatical.

Initially, I questioned this new impulse, fearing I was regressing or losing my way. In those moments of questioning, I was likely falling prey to the false belief that, once a person realizes Source, they remain detached and separated from the world at large and the tumult of modern life. However, I came to see that the inclination I felt drawn to follow was actually in alignment with what Ramana was teaching me — to trust my relationship with Source and to follow its direction, which is how I define intuition.

I initially questioned the aspiration because I simply was having a hard time imagining a life that did not include continuing to be a hermit — just like him.

And yet ...

After years of living as a monk and communing readily with Source, I felt strongly moved to re-engage with a worldly life and to explore how to integrate the realization of Source more directly into my dormant but still existent personality — with all her roles and desires still present in the background. I felt called to leave my hermitage and become a citizen of the world once again.

Recalling my original intent from back in my twenties — to live a meaningful life — I now sensed that a relationship with Source truly was the key to enacting that life. Though the option to stay in my cave with Source was compelling, I had a hunch that my experience needed to be *applied* in order to unleash the depth of fulfillment it promised — and which I longed for.

At this stage of my journey, I realized that hanging out in Source on my meditation cushion until I died would constitute a missed opportunity for something even more beautiful. After all, it was the personality — the Self — who was seeking meaning, not Source.

I became inspired.

I considered that maybe I *could* sustain a steady connection to Source *and* live a conventional human life. With that connection intact, what might I do? Who might I become? I imagined myself — and maybe others — benefiting from this powerful relationship in ways I would never know until I tried.

It took a few more years in retreat for me to sort out how to approach this phase of my life — and, admittedly, to bolster my courage to leave my simple and comfortable existence. But at the age of forty-two I felt confident that this integration of Source and Self was my destiny.

It was time to re-enter the world.

From that moment onward, living a life devoted to the weaving of Source and Self into one tapestry has been my north star. In the process of making my way in society, I felt inclined to organize my experience into a system that would help me stay on track and, as it turned out, would help others to find their way, too. I named this system Selfistry — a word that points to the alchemy of a Self in right relationship with Source — the Artistry of the Self.

Selfistry offers a potential story line for seekers that goes something like this ...

It's the Self who begins the search for a better life — often as a longing to decrease personal or collective suffering. As the Self seeks its answers, it will inevitably find its way to Source, the wellspring of its longing. With the assistance of a cultivated Witness awareness, the Self can learn to consciously integrate its experience of Source into a dynamic and evolving expression of selfhood ... ultimately generating a meaningful life, regardless of circumstance.

Selfistry maps the structure of this integrated selfhood into a framework with three Realms — Source (essential nature), Self (human identity), and Witness (conscious awareness). This trinity is the bedrock of Selfistry, carrying the fundamental guiding principles for enacting a meaningful life. People interested in Selfistry's approach are encouraged to look at themselves through the lens of these Realms.

In offering a map for exploring what makes us human, Selfistry also lays the foundation for discovering one's inner compass. This inner compass not only helps us orient among the Realms, it becomes the grounded center within, from which we can move gracefully in the world and make good decisions.

Finally, Selfistry offers practices as suggestions for exploring the depth and breadth of the territory. The practices presented are few, as there are already so many options to draw from in the expansive library of psycho-spiritual tools available. Novel techniques are not what are needed, but instead the reapplication of time-honored tools to a more up-to-date and relevant objective. Selfistry recognizes the benefit of individuals using the practices and techniques that resonate with them and that apply to the exploration of each Realm.

Exploration in the Realms yields growth and healing in all aspects of our human existence. The interplay among the Realms is what generates our skillful actions in the present moment and is what I call Artistry. Artistry matures as we consciously weave our personal destiny into the mystifying and ever evolving story of life itself.

THE WITNESS

Awaken your inner awareness.

We begin with the Realm of the Witness — the heart of Selfistry. This is the first Realm within Selfistry's trinity that we'll consider, as it provides a stable foundation for exploring the other two. By awakening an internal perceiver of ourselves, we create the conditions for ending the dominion of our personality as we have known it — an identity that tends to enslave us to habitual behaviors and beliefs. In addition, the Witness is well-positioned to assist us in rebooting our relationship with Source.

Let's start off with a story — one that originated in the ancient Indian subcontinent and has been widely diffused ever since — a story you may already be familiar with.

SELFISTRY

A group of blind men heard that a strange animal had come to town. It was an elephant. None of them were aware of the elephant's shape or form, so they began to explore it with their hands. Each blind man touched the part of the elephant closest to him.

When asked to describe what the elephant was, each spoke about the part they were touching. One said an elephant is like a thick snake — his hands were on the trunk. Another was certain that an elephant is like a fan — his fingers stroking the elephant's ear. And so on.

Each blind man was convinced they knew the entire elephant based upon their experience of the small part they were touching, regardless of what any of the others claimed.

Here's where the story goes in one of three directions — depending on who's retelling it.

The blind men hold onto their individual certainties and argue about what an elephant is.

The men share their points of view, possibly agreeing to disagree, and then go back to their homes with differing stories about elephants.

Or they somehow realize they were each touching a part of one whole animal and work to coordinate their perspectives into a bigger view, describing the elephant in its wholeness *and* its parts.

I prefer the third option because it illustrates an honest and complete experience of what it may be like to actually know something.

Granted, it would help if there were a sighted man in the story, able from the very beginning to orient the blind men to the bigger thing they were all touching.

But sometimes we need to find our way in the dark.

Now, imagine that you could enter the story and simultaneously be one of the blind men *and* a sighted person able to observe the entire event.

It's a bit of a stretch to imagine yourself as simultaneously both, but try not to limit this exploration to the questionable competency of your rational frontal lobe in these matters. Employ your imagination as well. Though it might take a bit of trial and error to learn how to perceive in such a way, our minds are truly mysterious — capable of far more than we've likely yet realized — and imagination has its own unique contribution to knowledge.

So stretch yourself. Go ahead. Ponder and putter a bit with your perception. Enter the story as an observer and a blind man. Imagine yourself caressing the elephant's thick wrinkled skin while you're watching from afar. Imagine the sensations on your fingertips as you see your hand from a distance. Toggle back and forth between the two perspectives.

Don't let yourself be discouraged by difficulty. After all, being yourself while also seeing yourself is not a simple maneuver — and certainly not a common one.

For eons, humans have preoccupied themselves with this challenge of seeing oneself objectively. Ontology is the branch of metaphysics that deals with the nature of being. Many mystics and philosophers have claimed that the ontological quest for true self-knowledge is inevitably adversely impacted by the fact that it's impossible for the human eye to see itself — which they ascribed as metaphorical evidence for humans' inability to know themselves objectively.

It's true — it is *physically* impossible for us to get outside of ourselves. It is also true that this incapacity impacts our ability to know ourselves. But only partially. Consider the simplicity of looking into a clear lake to see the reflection of your face or, with the invention of mirrors and cameras, seeing your own eyes pretty much as others see them. We're obviously seeing ourselves and gaining insight into who we are. While it's still true we will never be able to look into our own eyes *with* our own eyes, the question remains: Is this feat essential for acquiring the sort of self-knowledge we are pointing towards?

The answer is no.

With regard to acquiring a useful self-knowledge, it's important that we strive to reflect on ourselves — to see ourselves as objectively as possible — but how we do that warrants the sort of consideration we are employing here. Do not assume that objectivity is relegated solely to the domain of cognition, or that it demands a distinct *other* as the object of perception. We can see ourselves objectively from the inside, too.

If you're feeling skeptical, I understand. However, I promise you, as mystifying as the mind is and as wild as it seems to be able to both be and see ourselves, we can be rigorous in our methods so that the process of obtaining our self-knowledge is empirically sound and well wrought sci-entifically — while not being bound by the limitations of reason.

Which is why imagination can help.

And so can metaphors.

Here's another story.

This tale shows us how to take two apparently incompatible perspec-tives and integrate them into a third, more thorough, observation and subsequent experience of our perceived reality. The difference between this story and the elephant story? This one employs perspectives we al-ready embody. After all, many of us have never touched an elephant.

Once upon a time, until the mid-sixteenth century, the general agree-ment among humans was that the sun revolved around the earth. When people woke up in the morning, the sun rose in the east and, at the end of the day, it set in the west. As the sun crept across the sky through any given day, it was human perception and consensus that the sun was moving and the earth was not.

You and I continue to have this experience today.

Then along came Polish astronomer Nicolaus Copernicus. He argued that the earth actually turned daily on its axis and revolved around the circumference of the sun in the course of a year. He claimed that the daily rotation accounted for the experience of sunrise and sunset and the gradual shifting of the earth's axis as it revolved accounted for the changing seasons.

This was a radical view — and one not initially well received. After all, it fundamentally challenged people's lived experience.

The disagreements with Copernicus' assertion were rooted in people's inarguable subjective experience. Humans do not *feel* the earth rotating on its axis. We do, however, experience the sun moving through the sky.

So which experience is telling the truth?

The answer is both.

We do not have to reject the truth of our *experience* of sunrise and sunset just because we *know* that the sun is not actually moving through our sky. We can include our very real experience along with the knowledge of a now broader understanding of the earth's relationship to the sun.

In this way, though we accept definitively the objective truth that the earth revolves around the sun and rotates on its axis, it's also true that we have a daily experience of sunrise and sunset. These two truths inform one another and need not cancel each other out, as if one is more valid than the other. On the contrary, the intermingling of them — which brings us into a fuller experience, one that transcends and includes each perspective — has the ability to enrich our understanding and experience of life.

Through these stories, we begin to appreciate the significance of stepping back and getting a broader point of view while also staying connected to our immediate experience. The key here is to not insist on one view being more valid than the other. This clarity is important to sustain as we apply it to the more complex and nuanced experience of knowing ourselves.

Just as the Copernican Revolution expanded our capacity to understand our lives by uncovering knowledge about our relationship with the solar system, awakening our ability to view ourselves objectively has the potential to expand our self-knowledge and to transform our relationship with ourselves and others.

Here's how.

In the same manner that the dissemination of Copernicus' astronomical discovery throughout the population changed humanity's worldview, eastern mysticism and modern neuroscience have the power to transform our current view of ourselves.

Neuroscience is a vast and evolving field. I claim no expertise in it — simply a fascination with what I continue to learn and how it reflects and corroborates my experience of myself. That said, I will do my best to convey what I have learned as I share how my understanding informs how we humans experience ourselves.

Simply put, science shows that the brain fires a variety of disparate impulses all at once — and does so continuously. Each impulse has its own unique message, and our biological mechanism filters and integrates them into functions and actions that create a sense of identity and that support our survival.

Therefore, when it comes to a sense of self or personal identity, there is no singular impulse that fires and expresses as "me." Sarah is a mysterious and complex construct — an experience that emerges out of the coordination of any number of neural impulses. In other words, scientifically there is no "reality" to Sarah within the brain function. Just as there is no "reality" to sunrise and sunset.

This, however, does not mean that Sarah is not a real aspect of the experience of myself. Just ask me if I have an experience of being somebody. Of course I do. However, what I once believed was absolutely real — my personal identity as Sarah — I now know is a subjective phenomenon lacking objective corroboration.

Sarah is like a phantom — a figment of my mind — the result of a conglomerate of neurons regularly firing, based upon my particular organism's genetic makeup, life history, and present-moment context.

Please, pause and consider this for a moment.

In the same way that Copernicus' assertion was initially disorienting for people in his time, the news regarding a phantom-like identity might be unsettling for many of us today. Understandable. After all, René Descartes, a French scientist and philosopher born a century after Copernicus, essentially codified the age-old belief that our true-self is anchored in the brain, as expressed through his famous statement, "I think, therefore I am." If you think about it, it makes sense.

Descartes' perception is not false.

Still, it is only partially true.

It's also true that the idea that our identity is more like an apparition than a solid stable entity can leave us wondering who we really are and whether we have agency or free will at all.

This wondering is a good thing.

As it turns out, this new perspective on our identity has the power to be catalytic, expanding the range of our human experience rather than limiting it. As questions that once preoccupied the mystics and philosophers have crossed over into the disciplines of science — neuroscience and cognitive science alike — our knowledge is being enhanced. These fields and their ongoing discoveries are bringing added depth and breadth to our understanding and experience of being human.

But these scientific discoveries do not necessarily reveal anything radically new. Instead, they confirm what some spiritual traditions have been teaching for millennia.

Though a novel notion for many of us modern folk, preoccupied as we are with our individuality and personal autonomy, the experience of what some eastern traditions refer to as *no-self* has been around for a very long time. It's what Ramana was pointing me towards: the realization that our personality is more akin to a cloak than a substantial object or being.

For those who fear this news might cause some sort of mental breakdown, rest assured that this knowledge hasn't hindered the sanity or quality of life for many people throughout human history. Most individuals with this awareness have managed to function responsibly, lovingly, and creatively while embracing the reality of *no-self*. As am I.

Here's why you're not likely to lose your mind.

Historically, the experience of *no-self* did not prevent people with this awareness from accepting and living the very real experience of a personal Self because they were told about the *no-self* from a very young age. Once evoked, the *no-self* experience actually provided an opportunity to expand their sense of being human, not diminish it — to include a broader landscape of additional elements regarding their humanity and thus engage in a more fulfilling and creative life.

Once we learn about this phenomenon, regardless of our age or upbringing, we too have the opportunity to embrace two seemingly contradictory yet legitimate perspectives and integrate them into one seamless experience of our personhood. With practice, anyone can embody the knowledge that there is no fixed Self *and* that there is an enduring experience of a Self.

Both realities were — and remain — true. For each of us.

The negotiation of integrating these two truths into our daily life is no different from finding our way to continually enjoying the experience of sunrise and sunset while knowing that the earth is moving, not the sun.

As you consider what I'm saying, and maybe even do some investigating on your own, perhaps you will come to see that simply contemplating the possibility of a Self coexisting with *no-self* is a worthwhile endeavor.

However ...

No matter how fascinating it may be to think and talk about the concept of *no-self*, *experiencing* this truth is essential to a lasting impact. An embodied knowledge of *no-self* is what unleashes its ability to radically transform our lives.

Meditation is one of the most reliable techniques to help bring about a sustained experience of *no-self*.

There are many forms of meditation, all with varying goals. The meditation practice I recommend in Selfistry is designed specifically to help you stand back from yourself and observe, creating the conditions for you to validate for yourself that there is *no-self*. It's called the Sit Down and Shut Up Meditation.

I named it this because, early on in my quest, when my mind was swimming in teachings and philosophies, a dear friend suggested that I stop looking outside myself for answers. He suggested I take a break from my incessant seeking and ceaseless rumination and just sit down, shut up, and listen for a while. This one suggestion proved invaluable. It set me on course to learn how to be still and quiet and — in the open space that silence and stillness provide — to begin to see myself. Later on we will apply this meditation practice slightly differently in order to enhance our Artistry, but for now, it's all about cultivating the Witness.

The practice is simple: I sit still and keep quiet. While doing this, I seek to become aware of what's happening in my interior. I observe my mental mayhem, notice my emotional waves, and feel my bodily sensations. I might even imagine each thought, emotion, and sensation as its own unique neural phenomenon.

The goal is to grow my capacity to stay still and quiet so that I can observe all of my internal impressions *without engaging with them.*

As I practiced, I came to see that my experience of an integrated Self started to deconstruct before my internal eyes. After all, which singular thought, feeling, or sensation defines me? There are so many — and they often conflict. Is there a me who decides which impulses to act on and which ones to suppress? There are so many — and some are shameful or even repulsive.

And then comes the question, "Who is the me who is watching"? The Witness is like an inner Copernicus, come to reveal a bigger picture of who we are — without denying or denigrating our sense of identity up till now.

To be clear, in Selfistry we meditate with no intention to change ourselves. This is an important distinction from many other meditation and
mindfulness techniques. There are loads of "manifest your highest self"
meditations in the marketplace, as well as numerous stress reduction
meditations. Nothing wrong with these. Sit Down and Shut Up is neither.

In Selfistry, we meditate principally to awaken the Witness in ourselves
in order to see clearly how our fixed sense of Self might be better understood as habitual neural firings that coordinate into habitual behaviors and beliefs. When practiced over time, this form of meditation
metaphorically — and perhaps literally — creates a new neural pathway
whose sole purpose is to be present and to observe.

The practice of awakening the inner Witness is like bringing in a sighted
man to help the blind men make sense of the elephant. It's like leaving
earth's gravitational pull in order to view the earth revolving around the
sun.

But before we get too far ahead of ourselves, let's have some straight
talk about the practice of Sit Down and Shut Up.

In the beginning of learning how to meditate in this way, I spent a lot of
time feeling frustrated. I battled with the pull to quit, hating to sit still,
feeling like a failure, and fearing I was wasting my life.

I stayed with it because I sensed that I was onto something. I forced myself to sit quietly for hours and even days on end, believing that more

time on the cushion was the answer. However, even with my fervent attempt and dedicated discipline, I struggled to stay put. It was much easier to get through by daydreaming. Witnessing was not happening at all.

In other words ...

I would sit there and think a gazillion random thoughts, planning imaginary projects or contemplating esoteric truths. As a reaction to my thoughts — or possibly as initiators of them — I would experience waves of emotion ranging from elation to misery. And then there were the physical sensations: intense pain in any number of places in my body screaming at me to get up and move.

In between the thinking, feeling, and sensing, I *might* touch into Witnessing the thinking, feeling, and sensing — but only for a few seconds. I knew that I was *supposed* to be Witnessing, but it was incredibly hard to do. I felt like I was asking a muscle to work that either I did not have or was so atrophied that resurrecting its function was hopeless.

However, over time, the practice and discipline paid off. The muscle began to awaken.

Slowly but surely, as I became more accustomed to sitting still and keeping silent, I would experience a bit more of the back and forth between Witnessing and thinking/feeling/sensing.

It was slow progress at first. But it was progress, nonetheless.

Initially, I made a deal with myself and decided to measure my success quantitatively — solely by my ability to stay seated on the cushion. I would set a timer for anywhere from five to sixty minutes, and neither move nor quit until the timer went off. Success meant remaining seated and being still regardless of what was going on internally. Unless you are experiencing profound physical discomfort or extreme psychological distress, I suggest you begin in the same fashion, with the same measure for success.

Once I was fairly good at staying put, daydreaming notwithstanding, I began to steadily apply the intention to restrain myself from giving in to following my thoughts, feelings, or sensations. I did this by challenging myself to keep my attention focused on my breath instead. I hoped to be able to let the busyness of my thoughts, feelings, and sensations recede into the background.

The breath is an ideal anchor for this internal pivot, as the breath is always present, requires no thought or will for it to function, and is directly connected to Source — the breath breathing us.

Once again, over time, I persevered.

I became able to rest my attention on my breath whilst my thoughts, feelings, and sensations ran uninterrupted in the background. I successfully resisted the urge to relinquish my attention to them or let them compel me to take any particular action.

Please note that I am not claiming — nor would I ever claim — that my mind got quiet. This is not what happened — and, in Selfistry, this is not the goal.

The neural network's job is to fire in the form of thoughts, feelings and sensations. It does its job quite well. What the Sit Down and Shut Up Meditation can do is awaken an awareness that is able to perceive the impermanence of the Self ... as the thoughts, feelings, and sensations recede into the background of our attention.

With continued practice, this awareness expands.

A byproduct of cultivating the Witness in this way is that, by undertaking a regular meditation practice, we are developing a very basic and valuable skill in and of itself: self-discipline. Discipline does not have to be off-putting. To be disciplined does not inherently mean doing something hard or uncomfortable — though the commitment to sustained practice of any action may prove difficult. Discipline simply means engaging in an activity regularly regardless of how we feel about it. In fact, it comes from the Latin *discipulus*, one who studies.

It's common knowledge that most learning happens through repetition and deepens over time. So consider self-discipline as your friend — a skill that will serve you well in many areas of your life. I see now how a quality of maturity was being cultivated in me through the discipline of meditating, even when my mind ran amok. A state of being that I'm now able to apply to many aspects of my life, discipline lives in me as a certain dignity.

Through a disciplined meditation practice, you will learn how to not get lost in your mind. You will be able to confidently watch it — as if you were a drone hovering above yourself.

Careful, though ...

As you gain distance from your experience of being solely the thinker, feeler, and doer, you may want to tinker with yourself and try to manipulate or control your thoughts, feelings, or actions. I must caution you. In the Self section we will look more closely at the nature of our thoughts, feelings, and sensations — their strengths and their limitations. Then, in the Artistry section, we will explore how to be intentional about which thoughts and feelings to act on rather than being driven or held hostage by any one of them. But for now, stay here with me in the Witness Realm.

Though it can be tempting to believe meditation will be the magic elixir that will finally change you into some ideal person, that won't happen. There are limits to what meditation can provide on the path of realizing our potential.

We all have a relentless well constructed identity that pervades our existence no matter what. Every time we get off our meditation cushion, there it is. Changing that identity is not our objective.

Just as the sun kept rising and setting no matter what Copernicus said, our sense of Self is persistent.

And that's okay.

The Witness will help us escape the grip of our limiting identity so we can focus on the business of unleashing a fuller expression of who we are ... in time.

THE SELF

Liberate and celebrate yourself.

Without some sort of intervention, we would likely spend our entire lives believing and acting on our thoughts, feelings, and sensations without ever considering their origin or value.

As noted in the previous section, most of what we act on are beliefs and behaviors embedded into our psyches and encoded in our neurology. Though we might tell ourselves we're behaving consciously — choosing our destiny or manifesting our reality — we're actually more like a robotic expression of conditioned impulses and reflexive reactions.

Welcome to the Realm of the Self.

Our purpose in exploring this Realm is to get intimate with the content located here and, in the process, to deconstruct the structure of our identity. We will identify and sort the makings of our experience of being a "me." Then, upon unraveling the matrix of thoughts, feelings, and sensations that go into generating our sense of selfhood, we will be prepared to explore how to more consciously engage with these elements in order to enhance the expression of ourselves.

In other words, in the Realm of the Self we carefully dissect ourselves, even though we already know there actually is no singular fixed Self to dissect. This is a good thing — to know this before diving in — for it is precisely *because* we know there's no fixed Self that we're able to explore this Realm with dispassion *and* compassion — and eventually with joy.

I recognize the conundrum here: If we know there is *no-self,* why bother deconstructing something that doesn't exist? Why not just accept that the Self is like a persistent phantom and focus on uncovering a more real sense of who we are, possibly located in the Realm of Witness or Source?

The answer, which was illustrated through the Copernicus metaphor, applies in this way ...

We must include in any complete and credible self-knowledge the entire range of our selfhood — phantoms included. After all, thoughts, feelings, and sensations are real experiences — and so is the subjective sense of being a Self. These real experiences must be investigated if we are to include them in the Artistry of the Self. Our identity doesn't disappear just because we see its relative realness — just as the sun keeps rising and setting even when we know it doesn't.

Therefore, whereas in the Realm of the Witness we learn how to cultivate the capacity to observe, in the Realm of the Self we learn how to identify, engage, heal, and celebrate the makings of the Self we have come to Witness.

The field of western psychology functions on the premise that identity is real — not relatively real as I am suggesting, but really real like the shirt on your back. The many branches of psychology define the Self in any number of ways, depending on the particular school of thought. However, in general, they all hold a common perspective that the Self is an experience of a unitary, autonomous being who is separate from others and experiences continuity through time and place.

Many psychologists would agree that this experience of yourself includes consciousness of your physicality as well as your inner character and emotional life — sometimes referred to as the ego. Thus they strive to assist humanity in making this identity healthy and whole, based upon their definition of health and wholeness.

As a rule, traditional western psychology does not tend to stray into the arena of people objectively seeing themselves, nor into exploring the supposition that the ego is only relatively real. This approach has been linked more often to eastern philosophies and their efforts to demystify the notion of a Self and introduce the experience of *no-self*. Broadly speaking, spiritual methods from the east seek to help the practitioner break the habit of believing in a fixed identity. Western approaches seek to enhance it.

With the rising popularity of yoga and mindfulness in the west, there is now some infiltration of eastern perspectives into various fields of western psychology. While some of these fields may include a budding interest in the human capacity to objectify the Self, these efforts are primarily in service to a continued focus on manipulating or rehabilitating the structure of the Self — not on dismantling it completely.

Strictly speaking, the area of study where, psychologically, east meets west is still young, and many theories and clinical data are lacking depth and longevity — leaving them inconclusive, unsubstantiated, and often confusing. A constructive collaboration between east and west is certainly possible through systems and philosophies that seek to integrate the two truths of Self and *no-self* into a broader reality. Success in this endeavor will be a significant contribution to humanity's future.

Meanwhile, this impasse can be disorienting for the seeker who's longing for a way to personally grow or heal, as the marketplace is crowded with self-proclaimed psychological experts and self-anointed spiritual gurus making grandiose claims about what is possible when east meets west. This is why taking your time to investigate this Realm is crucial.

Make no mistake — learning how best to understand and care for one's psyche is complicated, and there is no single right way to do so. Mental health is more of a process than a steady state, which is why a sincere dedication to the study of one's own interior landscape is key, and why some confusion and disorientation are inevitable when it comes to making sense of what's inside.

Selfistry welcomes the use of any psychological tactic or tool for self-exploration that can aid in cultivating a healthy relationship with our interior. Identifying and expressing all the constituents of our personality is what we're after, and is what brings uniqueness and texture to our individual personhood. That said, it's important to remember that the Realm of the Self will never be granted sole proprietorship over our full human expression. The Self is simply one of three Realms and our full expression depends on the integration of all three.

As we proceed, feel free to substitute the word psyche or mind for "Self."

When mapping the Realm of the Self, it's important to know your vantage point, which means to differentiate between the experience of *seeing* yourself (the Witness' view) and the experience of *being* yourself. In other words, when the map says "you're here," there must be a "here" *within* your identity as well as one *outside* of it.

In general, western maps of the Self are derived solely from views within the Realm of the Self. In Selfistry, the perspective of the Witness, which stands *outside* the Realm of the Self, is critical to a comprehensive map of the Self. You can come to learn about yourself by having experiences of objective perception gathered from the Realm of the Witness, and you can discover the specific content that makes up your sense of a fixed Self from within the Realm of the Self. It happens that the content in the Realm of the Self is much easier to sort and celebrate when we can step outside of it every once in a while.

So what exactly *is* inside the Realm of the Self?

A lot!

To be more specific, the Self Realm contains *all* of your personality constituents — made from your unique mental, emotional, and physiological material.

Most western psychological schools refer to these distinct elements or traits and their concomitant behaviors as parts. After all, if psychologists begin with the premise that we exist as a whole Self, then it makes sense that, in order to accomodate the complexity of our interiors, they would describe us as having various parts.

For example, when you find yourself indecisive, you may say, "Well .... a part of me wants to do *x*, but another part of me wants to do *y*." Selfistry recognizes the identification and labeling of these parts as being integral to our discovery process. However, we do not refer to our inner tendencies as parts. We call them Selves.

We grant each part its own separate personality and call each one a Self because, when we investigate, each thought or feeling often does have its own backstory. By seeing them as unique beings, we organize our interior into more of a community rather than a bunch of disparate pieces. You'll find as you explore this approach that your parts actually organize willingly into mini yous, happy to have their voices heard and valued. Plus — as you will see — treating them as separate characters makes Artistry much easier to enact.

At first blush, this may seem weird — to call each part of you a Self. But when I changed this one term — early on in my retreat journey — I immediately felt space open up inside of me for a more multidimensional and complex experience of myself. In addition, altering the neuro-linguistics around how I spoke about myself helped loosen my identification as a fixed whole Self, making room for a relaxed experience of *no-self*.

This framework — isolating parts into separate autonomous mini identities and calling them Selves — is not unique to Selfistry. The mystic and philosopher G. I. Gurdjieff used it in his psychological views, as did the psychiatrist Carl Jung. Still, it is not a common approach.

To take parts and give them essentially their own selfhood can initially feel destabilizing when we're used to identifying as one whole identity with various components.

For many of us raised in the west, our belief in an undivided identity is so strong that to consider its non-fixedness — let alone its essential non-existence — can be viewed as a joke. Moreover, the suggestion that we dissect this identity into separate and multiple internal personalities can be seen as ridiculous — or even as a psychological disorder of its own.

This is unfortunate, as a healthy deconstruction of our identity is essential to any real and complete self-knowledge. American spiritual teacher, psychologist, and author Ram Dass refers to the stage of deconstructing one's identity as *Nobody Training*. This is in contrast to the phase of our lives from birth onward where we are appropriately preoccupied with "somebody training." If an outside force doesn't come in and disrupt our "somebody training," we're destined to believe we are somebody for the duration of our lives.

It's important to note that other voices within the New Age spiritual movement are not as clear as Ram Dass. Few western teachers maintain the purity of the eastern teachings as beautifully as Ram Dass did, where the intention is to do nothing to the ego or personality other than to see it for what it is.

By viewing ourselves from the perspective of the Realm of the Witness, the clarity that Ram Dass speaks of is available to us.

Selfistry maps the Witness in a Realm separate from the Realm of the Self because it's not enough to *know* we are fundamentally not a fixed identity. We must have an *embodied experience* of observing ourselves from a distance, which the Witness provides. To do so, we must leave the Self Realm and enter another.

Though the Witness may feel like a Self, it is not — not in the way we are defining and describing the Selves in the Realm of the Self. It will serve us well if we keep this distinction stable. The Witness is the experience of a universal, objective, and loving awareness — the same in each of us and not unique to any one individual.

It's true that, as we awaken the Witness and encounter its awareness, we will have the experience of "I am aware." However, the "I" is referring to the location of awareness arising in our human form and not to any personal identification or ownership.

The Witness has no impulse to do anything other than to observe. Its sole purpose is to be present and aware, regardless of external circumstances.

Selves have agendas.

The Witness does not.

Once you begin to explore the Realm of the Self, you'll see your Selves and their agendas more clearly. Most of us have a handful of Selves who are especially strong and who continually run the show. They can be explained as the specific neural firings that are nearly always included in the physiological process of generating our identity. Or we might view them as the habitual pattern our brain settles into in order to accomplish our "somebody training." Some people view these Selves as learned behaviors introduced early on by parents or caregivers, past life karma, or genetic dispositions.

Regardless of the tale we weave about their origin, whenever we remain fixated with any repetitive pattern, we lock into an identity wherein any other peripheral Selves or weaker signals may never get expressed. We function under the belief that we are who we think we are while those marginalized Selves get buried in our subconscious — sometimes emerging in dreams or psychological distress.

As we accept the reality that we are not the fixed identity we have taken ourselves to be, we begin to notice and isolate the specific behaviors and beliefs that have defined our selfhood up until now. We then begin to notice the weaker signals as well — the desires and beliefs we have not allowed ourselves to experience or express. If we treat each tendency as a Self and get to know them intimately, discovering their backstories and their withheld longings, a whole new world opens up for us.

Over time you'll discover ways to keep your particular community of Selves from going underground again and may even discern how to heal them, if needed. As you increase your capacity to Witness and not act instantly on any given impulse, you will be prepared to meet each Self and employ them all in the fullest expression of you. As you proceed, the loudest ones will no longer have the mandate to solely run the show.

Here's an example.

Imagine you're in a fight with your partner regarding money. You are very familiar with the flavor of this fight, as you've been here in two previous relationships. You are the primary breadwinner for the family and feel that your partner is spending more money than you'd prefer. They work part-time and do most of the child and home care.

Together you go to a couples therapist. The therapist invites you to express yourself and requests that you be fully honest. You start explaining how you keep asking your partner to limit their spending — as your blood pressure rises along with your voice. You're yelling. You're angry. Scared. Feeling out of control.

The therapist asks you if you're aware that you're angry.

"Of course!" you shout. "Isn't it obvious?!"

The therapist acknowledges your courage for telling the truth and thanks you for expressing your feelings.

The therapist then invites your partner to share their experience and express their feelings, and maybe you have a moment of hearing each other. As a result, some couples might have a reprieve from the stressful dynamic for a while. However, the reprieve is not enough to change the pattern.

Most couples never break their patterns.

Now imagine you've been taught a new way to view yourself. You've started a meditation practice whose focus is on cultivating the inner Witness. You're becoming able to access a place inside yourself from where you're able to observe yourself with spacious awareness.

Then the credit card bill arrives and you freak out.

The first thing you do is *notice* that you're freaking out. You have enough awareness to know that a Self is highly triggered. You do not rage at your partner — or at your kids or the credit card bill. Instead, you may go outside and scream, allowing the rage to be released from your mind and body. Then you sit down and check in with the Self who is freaking out.

You are not freaking out. A Self *in you* is freaking out.

This is a radically transformative experience.

As you enter the therapist's office, you are calmer. When the therapist asks you what's up, you speak with noticeable objectivity and sincerity. You talk about the Self inside you who you're getting to know intimately. You tell the therapist how that Self felt that her family never had enough money while growing up. You describe how you watched your father always freak out about finances.

With a calm and regulated nervous system, you ask the therapist to help you and your partner navigate your relationship to money in a way that takes into consideration all the different Selves inside each of you — because you know for sure there is also a Self in you who wants your partner to buy whatever they need and another Self who is excited to make more money.

Now imagine if your partner had this same awareness and way of knowing themselves. And imagine that, all along, they'd been struggling with a Self inside of them who felt frozen when it came to spending money that they had not earned. As a result, they were buying only what they felt were minimum necessities — ashamed that they were not able to contribute more fully to the family expenses and resentful they did not have more of what they wanted.

Without this awareness, your partner might be looking to act out, to escape, or possibly even to break up the family. With this awareness, they would likely be able to express their shame and explore all the inner Selves activated in the partnership dynamic. Which Selves have been getting triggered? What do they need?

Now imagine what the conversations between the therapist and the couple might sound like, moving forward.

With this degree of self-awareness, self-knowledge, and ability to communicate with one another, the therapist becomes a Witness and guide. The therapist might not even be needed.

Granted, this example may read as an oversimplification of the actual lived complexities of our intimate relationships. However, the richness and spaciousness that increasingly emerge via the process of knowing oneself and one another, illustrated through this example, are real, powerful, and transformative.

The Realm of the Witness is where we access a quality of awareness that is capable of making space for all our Selves to be seen and heard. When we navigate with the assistance of the Witness, we are able to draw from all the Selves and allow for the entire cast of characters to find their place in a fuller expression of our being human.

Over time, you will find yourself no longer subject to the ingrained fixed identity patterns that were generated in you early on. The best news is you will never have to make those Selves wrong — nor will you need to get rid of them, change them, or go out and get new ones.

This is key.

There is no need for you to remake yourself into an idealized version of you. The components of the best version of you already exist inside you.

Selfistry's viewpoint is that we step into the journey of seeking to become whole already complete. It's a conundrum, I know. But the truth is, you are neither broken nor lacking. Selfistry is merely assisting you in expanding and enhancing the expression of yourself as you are. It's true that, in the process of remaking yourself, you may do some rearranging, but you never tear yourself down and start over. The process is more like a recalibration or renovation.

The beauty of this approach is that every aspect of you remains welcome and is included in your unique ever-emergent expression of your humanity — generating an abiding sense of peace and satisfaction.

No Self gets buried or exiled.

Ever.

No Self gets to always run the show.

Ever.

With the help of the Witness and Source, internal angst and struggles with conflicting Selves get seen, resolved, and integrated. This process is not always without challenge but, over time, decisions about how to act become easier to make. Opposing Selves who were once polarized get to know one another and find ways to accommodate each other over the course of your life.

Do not, however, imagine that your internal landscape eventually quiets down. Though the particulars evolve over time, the Realm of the Self is always fairly crowded and noisy — for everybody. Selves constantly appear, act, retreat, and re-emerge. Some grow and change while others stay the same. The practice in this Realm is to continually meet and greet all of them.

The specific methods used for Self exploration and the tools designed to help call Selves forth will vary from person to person. A few methods I have found effective for ongoing discovery are certain forms of therapy, journaling, visualization, and sacred theater or role play.

Journaling is a classic way of tending to our relationship with ourselves. Now you can use this tool to inquire and explore intimately and privately with each Self. You may opt to journal with words, images, voice, or movement — captured in writing, art, recordings, or video. In addition, when investigating alongside others or in community, you can experience and observe your Selves through role play, experimenting with improvisational expressions of the various Selves for one another.

When I ponder the often overwhelming content of the Self Realm, I find comfort in imagining that, when the Buddha spoke of suffering, he may have been pointing to the suffering inherent in being held hostage by any one Self from within the Realm of the Self. Some translations of the Noble Truths in Buddhism say that the root of suffering is *desire*. However, I have found that suffering exists only when I am *bound* by desire and have no capacity to step back and see desire for what it is — a natural expression of one or more of my Selves.

When I nurture this understanding, knowing that I have a way to no longer be bound by any one desire, I feel free. Though Selves may at times be fierce and relentless, with a stable footing in the Realm of the Witness and a strong connection to Source, desires are free to arise. I do not have to act on them. They can remain in my being without governing my actions. Some desires will get met. Some won't. No problem. And thus no suffering.

The House Visualization

A Selfistry practice specifically designed for exploration of this Realm is called the House Visualization. In this practice, I invite you, once again, to recruit your imagination to help you come to know your Selves.

Visualization techniques orient the mind in a particular direction to assist in achieving a desired result. In this case, you ask your mind to imagine yourself as a house or dwelling place, with the intention to enter it and discover the Selves living inside.

Begin by getting your body comfortable in a quiet place and closing your eyes or softening your gaze. Imagine yourself walking along a road or trail somewhere in nature as you come upon a dwelling. As you approach the structure, you are aware that you will be entering into an imaginary place where you will meet yourself. When you open the door, you encounter a full house of Selves.

Upon entering the house, you investigate the various floors and rooms as you encounter the Selves located there. They will likely show up as being different ages, doing various activities — basically living out their stories before your imaginal eyes. There is no right or wrong way for you to explore what you encounter or to engage with those you meet.

Spend as much time as you wish with your Selves before finding your way back to the trail and returning to the present moment. Complete the practice by harvesting your experience through sharing with a friend or journaling.

Each visualization session is unique, in that different Selves come forward at different times. The most important element of this exercise is setting aside the time to slow down and be with yourself — to discover what's inside. Over time, with a regular practice, you will familiarize yourself with the consistent cast of characters who inhabit your house and become comfortable with new ones as they appear. As you cultivate a relationship with each of them, you increase your Self knowledge and thus your capacity for a fuller expression of yourself.

In addition, through setting aside time for a recurrent practice of self-reflection, you become increasingly able to access and observe your Selves in real time, leaving you less reactive and more responsive in most situations. Under duress, any number of Selves are likely to be activated, yet none of them will likely be the sole one you'll want to take direction from. The ability to pause and be present will bring forth numerous options for action. As we saw in the example earlier about the couple in therapy, over time you will have at your disposal many creative possibilities for navigating your life's challenges.

The ability to pause and observe creates the conditions for wise and courageous acts to be taken. Reactivity diminishes.

Once you're comfortable with the visualization process, you can expand the House Visualization to include the Realm of Witness in the following way.

The basement of the dwelling, the attic, or even the periphery is where the Realm of the Witness can be found. Once you arrive in your chosen location — a place from which you can see the entire dwelling — imagine the floors and walls in the house turning to glass so that you can simply observe the cacophony of the Selves comfortably from a distance.

It helps to visualize a super comfy chair in the Witness space ready for you to settle in and relax. Once settled, imagine yourself watching your house full of Selves with spacious awareness. No need to engage with any of them.

. . .

Regardless of what tools or techniques you use to explore the Realm of the Self, it's important to remember two things.

First, in addition to adding on a Witness vantage point in the House Visualization, make sure you continue doing the Sit Down and Shut Up Meditation — or whatever technique you have discovered that works for you to cultivate the Witness. It's regenerative to regularly take time to simply rest as the Witness — observing the Selves without talking to them or taking any action in response to them.

Second, as you begin to slowly invite the Selves to come forward and speak — to show and share themselves, take your time. There is no rush — they're not going away.

The Realm of the Witness was introduced first so that, when you explore the Realm of the Self, you always have a place you can go to rest, pause, stand back, and observe. In this way, you will become more present and grounded in general, and the Selves will be more likely to stand down or to willingly come forward. Sensing a loving presence Witnessing them, the Selves begin to trust they will not be exiled, judged, shamed, or bullied.

The inevitable outcome of accepting our Selves without judgment is that we liberate silenced voices and longings. We grant permission for hidden Selves and their desires to come forward and be heard.

What this looks like in real life is that you are no longer bound by habits or patterns that stifle or derail you. To be clear, they may arise now and then, but they will no longer be the only habits or patterns that get to express themselves.

You are no longer ashamed of longings that might not be socially acceptable or do not fit into your family of origin's idea of who you should be. The shame-filled Self is still present, but it no longer blocks those legitimate longings from coming forward. The shame-filled Self gets to feel its shame, but it does not get to silence the longings or actions of other Selves.

You also become less afraid to try something new or to meet an unfulfilled desire. While there are certainly Selves in each of us who are afraid, there are also Selves who are not. Over time, you become more able to allow the fearful Selves to be present without letting them dictate your actions. You relax more deeply into the magnificence of your unique assortment of Selves as you prepare to more intentionally coordinate them into an expression of your full potential.

On the one hand, through entering the Realm of the Self, you're fully exposed — likely shocked or embarrassed by some of what you discover. This is not uncommon. On the other hand, through this process, you meet yourself in all your magnificence as well. Ultimately you come to accept all your Selves. You stop trying to be somebody other than who you already are.

Note that, in the process of liberating the Selves in this Realm, you will likely come upon Selves who need special attention or healing. Some of them may be traumatized or frozen and will need help to become available for Artistry. Thus certain therapeutic interventions may be advised.

This leg of your journey will have to be catered to your specific Selves and their needs. Additional support may include hiring a therapist, stepping into a recovery program, working with a psychiatrist, or engaging in other spiritual or somatic techniques. These and other tools are welcome and encouraged.

To recap ...

The Witness awakens by turning your attention away from the Realm of the Self.

The Realm of the Self becomes available for Artistry when you turn your attention towards it to meet, allow, and liberate all of your Selves.

If the Witness is the observing awareness, acting as a loving space of acceptance without an agenda, then the question arises: Who or what will coordinate the Selves into Artistry?

The answer lies not in any one Self or in any one Realm. Artistry happens when all three Realms are active and existing in harmony with each other.

Therefore, it's time to introduce the third Realm.

SOURCE

Reclaim the sacred and miraculous.

Welcome to the Realm of Source. This is where we awaken our personal experience of the essential reality that we humans are rightfully inclined to experience as miraculous, and which is often called God.

We've already examined the nature of our personal identity residing in the Realm of the Self and have laid the groundwork for embracing and embodying the two perspectives of Self and *no-self* with the help of the view from the Witness Realm. Now it's time to remember and to underscore that we are ultimately and eternally incomprehensible beings — no matter what we find in any Realm and no matter what anybody says to the contrary.

Whether you presently orient to the Realm of Source from the perspective of science or religion, mysticism or pragmatism, agnosticism or atheism, does not matter. The beauty and majesty of Source is that it is not bound by our human perceptions or stories about it. It is perpetually true to itself, allowing us to entertain our perceptions as we wish.

The key to approaching this Realm is to reclaim a sense of wonder.

Recall Ramana's teaching where the self-inquiry process eventually uncovers the realization of our essential nature? Remember my experience of meditating for so many years that eventually I dissolved into a spacious and vast mystery? This is the experience we're after here.

However, we have some preparation to do. First, we will identify our current ideas and beliefs about this Realm. After that, we will be free to update or add to those beliefs. Finally, we will set aside all our stories about Source in order to have a genuine experience of it, unfettered by any ideas.

Source can be defined as an incomprehensible presence that is always accessible to us, regardless of our life circumstances, the way we were raised, or what we were taught to believe. Though access to this fundamental sense of being may feel out of reach, the truth is that it's never inaccessible and it doesn't have to take years of practice to uncover.

All of us carry stories about Source that can block us from having a pure encounter. Not a problem. Selves are meant to have stories, especially about the origin and purpose of life. They need them in order to make sense of themselves. However, in this Realm, our intention is to take stock of those stories in order to then set them aside and make room for a storyless experience.

Let's begin by exposing a couple of stories that you're likely carrying and may not be aware of. These stories are embedded in the three primary monotheistic religions and are the bedrock of spiritual belief in the western world. The first conviction is that God is above, before, and/or better than "his" creation — which includes us. The second is that we need an intermediary to connect with this omnipotent God.

In general, adherents of Judaism, Christianty, and Islam do not encourage us to seek a personal connection to Source. They suggest we leave that job to Moses, Jesus, or Mohammed and their direct disciples or prophets, and then just do as they say. Even though the most progressive offshoots in these three religions may speak to cultivating a personal relationship with God, it's usually in the context of God already having been defined and the pathway to him prescribed. In all three monotheistic lineages, the persistent message — blatant or subtle — is some version of this: We are born from sin, God is our savior, and we better follow the rules if we want to fix what's broken and get to some version of heaven when we die.

Let me be clear: I mean no disrespect.

Christianty, Judaism, and Islam all carry a stockpile of goodness, truth, and beauty in their teachings and their ways of guiding humans to living meaningful lives. Plus, I'm fairly certain that all three have root teachings that once sought to align and connect each of us personally to the divine — all of us being worthy *just as we are*. But few of us today are aware of these esoteric threads, let alone benefit from them. Though they may have their origins in clear wisdom paths, many branches of the Jewish, Christian, and Muslim religions have gone mildly to wildly astray, leaving many people disoriented when it comes to a living an authentic spiritual life.

We certainly can learn a lot from the religious beliefs, spiritual practices, and theological philosophies that have existed throughout human history, and I suggest we do so. However, what's important to understand with regard to this Realm is simply that most of us are starting off with an imposed, tentative, or confused relationship with this thing we've historically called God.

Many of us aren't even aware of how the foundational assumptions embedded in our families and societies inform or distort a clear view of our spirituality, whether or not our families were adherents of any religion or specific spiritual orientation. These unconscious worldviews affect us in many ways, so pernicious are their subtle influences.

This is not to say that we can or should throw religion away or start over and create new ones. Our collective human history and unique ancestral lineages have much beauty and wisdom present in them for us to benefit from and carry forward. It would be foolish to start from scratch. We simply could benefit from doing some sorting — some serious exploration of our unconscious beliefs — and then updating our views to reflect our lived experience in the present time.

When we explore this Realm with patience and curiosity, something transformative becomes possible. As someone who spent more than a decade devoted to understanding and penetrating the Realm of Source, I believe the bulk of our global challenges would be solved if everyone rebooted their relationship to Source. Same is true with regard to our personal problems. After all, it was my direct relationship to Source that brought me back into the world and helped me face my personal challenges with an open mind and heart.

As you proceed, be gentle yet thorough in the unearthing of your long held unconscious assumptions about this Realm. To help, here's an additional detail that may be of interest: There's another possibly more useful spiritual story in our midst that you may not be aware of. It's a welcome alternative to the ones we're more familiar with and just might help light your way.

This alternate story speaks to the sacred essence of our existence without any need to define it or to seek an intermediary in order to know it. This story has been told since the beginning of recorded human history. Monotheism is actually a relatively new story. This more ancient tale is sometimes called the perennial philosophy. It basically says that nothing, no being or thing, is separate from its Source. Another way of saying this is that the spiritual and the material co-arise. Neither is superior. In other words, whether or not we *believe* this to be so, the perennial wisdom claims we are simultaneously divine and mortal. Said another way, we are both God and human or, in Selfistry terms, Source and Self.

I suggest you not take in what I'm saying solely through your rational mind, for you will likely dismiss it. Instead, if you open your imagination and expand your capacity to wonder, some other form of understanding might be catalyzed. Consider what these words are pointing towards rather than the literal interpretation of them, which will inevitably fall short.

The perennial philosophy strips away any anthropomorphizing of the holy mystery and leaves us with the primal experience of the paradox of our human condition.

Paradox: a seemingly absurd or contradictory proposition which, when investigated, may prove to be founded or true.

Paradoxes are not meant to be rationally understood; they are meant to be inhabited. Lived.

Once again, let's return briefly to our Copernicus analogy to help us learn how to grok any paradox — but especially the divine and mortal one.

As a species, we've come to accept the very real experience of sunrise and sunset while also knowing that the earth is the object moving, not the sun. Is this not itself an example of inhabiting two seemingly absurd or contradictory propositions that, when investigated, can be embraced into one more comprehensive gestalt?

Now I'm asking you to deploy this very same ability towards the seem-ingly contradictory propositions regarding our humanity and our divinity. Can we simultaneously experience ourselves as mortal individuals and know ourselves as something else as well?

Let's imagine our human experience as analogous to our experience of sunrise and sunset — where we live the very real experience of being born (sunrise) and dying (sunset). If our individual lives are the sunrise and sunset, what is the equivalent corollary to the earth rotating on its axis?

The answer is — from the perspective of Source, nothing is born or dies. They just appear to rise and fall, just as the sun appears to rise and fall.

From the view of Source, Source is all there is.

How can this be? How can we know for certain Source is all there is, as we know for certain that the earth rotates on its axis?

Some would argue that we can't ever know for certain objectively. In other words, we can't literally get outside of ourselves in order to view ourselves as Source in the way that launching a rocket from Earth allows us to validate the earth's rotation.

Unfortunately, as helpful as they are in orienting us, metaphors can only take us so far. The truth of ourselves as Source having a human experience can only be realized in oneself.

Rest assured, despite their limitations, talking and thinking about this paradox is not a waste of our time. Doing so can help to orient us. Similarly, acknowledging that Source is truly a mystery is not a copout. It does not mean that Source is not significant, enduring, or real in the way that the earth rotating on its axis is real. It simply means that we must know its realness without needing to understand it logically.

Fully inhabiting this paradox — integrating our lived experience as mortal individuals into an equally true experience of ourselves as an eternal mystery — has the promise of radically transforming us ... setting us free to become a different kind of human.

In order to do so, we must open ourselves up afresh to the unknowable, meet mystery as it is, and not turn away or collapse it into something knowable.

Describing the mystery through stories is what humans have always done. It's understandable. It's how we make sense of the seemingly nonsensical. The problem arises when the stories themselves are believed to be truth rather than reflections of the incomprehensible reality they are pointing at. When a story crystallizes over time into dogma rather than reflecting or amplifying the mystery — or worse, intentionally distorts it — then we know it's time for a new version of the story.

The mystery, however, remains constant.

In Selfistry, we recognize and even celebrate that the fundamental paradox of our existence is the dynamic interplay between the Realms of Self and Source. The Witness Realm, which holds our conscious awareness, helps us to stand back in order to see this paradox. When we're able to relax our rational mind and inhabit this paradox, moving in and out of our experience as a Self and as Source, a creative power is unleashed.

We are always and eternally this paradox, whether we realize it or not. However, when we become a conscious living expression of this paradox in our day-to-day lives, a new way of being human is available to us.

Therefore, our intention in this Realm is to reclaim the experience of ourselves as pure Source.

When we enter the Realm of Source, any sense of Self is completely subsumed. This is the experience of *no-self* that Ramana refers to. It is the Emptiness that Buddhism refers to, the Tao in Taoism, the Ain Soph in Kabbalah. It has many names, all representing one truth.

In the Realm of Source, our human mortality is brought into perspective and is no longer something to bemoan or fear. From within this Realm, the relative reality of birth and death are embraced within a bigger view.

Eventually this realization brings insights regarding how our impermanent individual human lives might express themselves before they expire (sunset). However, in the beginning, our dissolution in the Realm can be disorienting and even frightening.

Not to worry.

Over time, you get used to it.

Soon the Realm of Source is where the Self regularly turns for inspiration and revelation — without an intermediary and without fear.

There's no shame in admitting that we're conditioned and likely confused about Source. In fact, it's a healthy confession, because when our uncertainty about this Realm is acknowledged, we then have an opportunity to begin again.

Beginning again means taking time out from the business of our human striving in order to contemplate the impermanence of our one precious and miraculous life. No matter what we believe or do, we — as we know and identify ourselves from within the Self Realm — will die. However, our experience of ourselves as mortal humans does not displace the reality that we are divine.

Though the experience of sunrise and sunset does not change, knowing the truth about the sun and earth changes your experience of sunrise and sunset. How could it not?

Similarly, though our experience of feeling separate from the divine may not change upon the realization of our Self as Source, the experience — the embodied knowledge — will certainly change how we navigate our one precious life. Again, how could it not?

Selfistry suggests a considered approach in achieving this discovery for yourself.

First, identify the Selves who hold particular spiritual worldviews and who often attempt to direct the course of your life based upon these stories. See them for who they are: storyholders. Listen to their stories. Pay them attention. This is taking inventory.

Next, uncover the Selves holding different views and questions about Source, and who've been silenced by the dominant Selves. Listen to their stories. Encourage them. Add them to your inventory.

Finally, embark on the adventure of having a brand-new experience of Source directly — no stories involved.

You can carry out the first two steps using the same tools suggested in the previous section discussing ways to meet the Selves — journaling using a chosen medium, or sacred theater.

Next, as you prepare to generate a fresh encounter with Source, Selfistry suggests a specific strategy to help guide your exploration. The strategy includes three avenues of approach: a third-person, a second-person, and a first-person orientation. Each of these perspectives reveals different facets of the Realm of Source and allows for a nuanced and rich experience for the Self.

In a third-person investigation, you approach Source from a detached and objective point of view, looking at the fields of religion and beliefs with a discerning and open mind. You might study texts written about Source or ask people what they believe and why. As you dig into the origins of belief systems and religions and how they impact our psyches, you will begin to identify a variety of spiritual worldviews and experiences available for consideration.

In a second-person investigation, you approach Source as an intimate other. Whereas in a third-person investigation you're seeking knowledge *about* Source from various references, in this approach you're seeking to hear directly *from* Source. For this exploration, you might imagine Source as some form of energy or as any particular image you favor. Just remember, Source is ultimately imageless. Generating an image of Source does not suggest that Source is a thing, not even energy. Your image is merely an impression employed to help you in your approach.

Ways of engaging this two-way relationship might be through song, prayer, poetry, or dance. The idea is to nurture a close relationship and ongoing dialogue with Source. It helps to not try to figure out how a relationship with Source is even possible and to simply allow for enchantment.

In a first-person relationship with Source, the intention is to allow your Self to dissolve into the Realm as you experience yourself *as* Source. This is what Ramana taught and is the goal of many other eastern spiritual technologies, as well as the target of mystics and saints in some western traditions.

In Selfistry, we're not looking to dissolve into Source forever; still, we *are* looking to have some time there. It's upon our emergence from this dissolution when we must be cautious. In the Self's effort to understand what it encountered there, it will begin to weave a story. But the experience is not the story. And the story is not the experience. The experience is key. The story is not.

To bring about a first-person experience of Source, you might employ the practices of meditation, visualization, or, in some cases, plant medicines or psychedelics.

I encourage you to not overthink the whole affair of dissolution or how you will ever manage to have the experience of communing with Source in such a way. Simply having the understanding that it is possible and that you are capable and worthy of it can change you. It may also help to know that, historically, an undisputed portal to experiencing Source directly is through stillness and silence — both of which are easily accessible to you at your bidding. Another readily available gateway is nature.

Exposure to stillness and silence is rare for most of us, given our society's addiction to incessant activity and sound. It can be hard to resist the seduction of continual doing. However, I encourage you to not imagine the experiences of silence and stillness to be boring. In fact, it's best to not imagine them at all. Employ your curiosity in being still and quiet and find out for yourself what they are and how they might benefit you.

Once experienced, I found that the quality of silence encountered in the Realm of Source served to magnify and clarify the sounds I heard in the world. The quality of stillness I found there offered a stability that remains capable of supporting the grandest movements of my Self.

Nature has its own style of pulling us out of ourselves and into the mystery. A sunrise, a hummingbird, or a forest all have the potential to scream at us, "Hey human, wake up! This whole thing is a miracle. Including *you!*"

Historically, shamans and mystics have tended to spend most of their time outdoors, using the natural world as a reminder and as a co-conspirator in slowing down and being quiet enough to access Source in themselves and in the world they inhabit.

Nature just might be your ideal entry.

Remember ...

No matter what avenues you take, your sincere efforts will surely serve you. For successful and enduring Artistry, a living relationship to this Realm is key. It helps to gain a clear understanding of what Source is and is not. It helps to feel comfortable approaching Source as an other, as well as dissolving into it. But more than anything, the value of this relationship being your own, cleared of past conditioning and imposed beliefs, cannot be overstated.

If you ever feel hopelessly blocked, attending to the breath is a great start. Sit down and simply breathe for a bit as you ask yourself this simple question: Who or what is the breath breathing me? This is equivalent to Ramana's question, *Who am I?* used in his inquiry method.

SARAH MARSHANK

In the Realm of the Witness, when we practice the Sit Down and Shut Up Meditation, we use the breath as a touch point to pull our attention away from fixating on the shenanigans of our Selves. This same practice can now be expanded to become a bridge to Source. By bringing your attention first into the Witness, you can then use that Realm as a portal into Source.

As you breathe, imagine yourself turning towards Source. Inquire, with repetition: What is the Source of this breath breathing me? As you move your attention farther away from the Self who is asking and breathing, you will forge a pathway for your attention to be captivated and dissolved into Source.

Without establishing a personal relationship to this holy mystery, you will be bound by the stories about Source that you've gathered in the Realm of the Self, recycling them over and over like *Groundhog Day*.

We all know how fun that is.

Your explorations in this Realm can be some of the richest experiences you will ever have. When you turn your attention away from the Realm of the Self, the miracle of who you are — paradoxically Self and *no-self* — appears effortlessly ... because it is always here.

Selves come and go.

Source remains.

ARTISTRY

Be the Artist and the Art.

Now is probably a good time to pause. Take a deep breath and feel your aliveness for a moment. Maybe close your eyes and simply rest in the experience of being breathed.

Wonder with me ...

How is it that so many of us have lost touch with the marvel of our very existence?

How is it that some of us feel so disconnected from the pure miracle of being alive that we take life for granted or feel justified in causing harm to others and to the planet?

Maybe we simply don't know ourselves well enough yet, or what we are capable of, or how to be fabulous humans in challenging times. Forgive me for sounding presumptuous or possibly naïve in suggesting that maybe we can change this. I just can't see doing anything with my life other than attempting to contribute to a future I imagine as possible.

And yet ...

No matter how certain I am of what I know, I'm clear that, regardless of the power of my beliefs or the credence of all I have learned, I can never escape the truth that nobody really knows for sure what life is, why we are here, or where we're headed.

We only know for certain that we are.

What's also irrefutable is that from this undeniable condition of aliveness has emerged billions of miraculous beings.

Equally indisputable is that you are one of them!

The uniqueness of who you are is stunning. Truly. There is no other like you. Nor will there ever be. Let this sink in. Feel yourself as a singular magnificent occurance in a miraculous and vast universe.

Your uniqueness began in utero — perhaps earlier — and continues to develop and evolve throughout your life and possibly into death. All that

Selfistry is attempting to do is to capitalize on your uniqueness, harness your innate human impulse to grow, and help you create a gorgeous version of you.

This is Artistry.

Artistry is our intentional engagement in deepening our embodiment of our Selves, the Witness, and Source. Though these three Realms are always present in us and intermingling, regardless of our awareness of them, our awareness changes everything. By applying awareness to our actions, we can begin to purposefully develop ourselves into the humans we long to become.

Let's briefly review what we've learned as we prepare to bring clarity on how to engage in successful Artistry.

We started with the Realm of the Witness, where we located our consciousness and, more specifically, an awareness capable of seeing ourselves objectively. We considered how to focus our attention on simply being aware — not conscious of anything in particular but alive as consciousness itself. We also recruited the Witness as an ally in helping us to embrace our *no-self*ness while calling our Selves forth.

Sometimes I refer to the Witness as the secret sauce of Selfistry because this simple act of pausing and stepping back is deceptively powerful in catalyzing change.

Next, I introduced the Realm of the Self, dedicated solely to housing our mortal human selfhood. Here is where we identify and celebrate our uniqueness.

In deconstructing the Self, we locate numerous different Selves involved in the makeup of our complicated matrix of selfhood. Though we likely came into this work experiencing ourselves as a fixed identity, we come to know the relativeness of this view. With the Witness offering us a reprieve from our habitual self-absorption, we become equipped to handle our Selves with more tolerance, compassion, and curiosity ... so that we may enlist them in our Artistry rather than allowing them to be in charge.

Finally, we presented the sacred paradox of that which simultaneously manifests as you and is the creator of you. Source will always remain a mystery and, as such, we acknowledge its special place in our lives. As for its role in Artistry, we recruit it to glean a meta perspective, to experience permission to be ourselves, and to remember how to live in awe and wonder. However, we do not elevate it in value above the Realm of the Self.

There is no hard evidence that formlessness is more holy than form or that God is more sacred than humans. Selfistry's perspective is that the transcendent and the immanent each play a significant role in the unfolding of all that is. The perspectives, insights, and experiences explored and harvested in the Realm of Source are invaluable to the process of becoming ourselves. By attending to this Realm, we see how much our relationship to Source impacts the overarching quality of our lives — as well as the nitty-gritty particulars.

As we examine what it looks like to become the Artist of your life, it can help to view Artistry not as something you do now and then, but as a way of living. Truly no aspect of our lives is left out of the Art. Ever. From bowel movements to washing dishes and even — maybe especially — dying, we bring all three Realms to bear on this endeavor.

To step into Artistry, we first acknowledge that there is an ongoing dynamic relationship among the Realms that is alive and emergent beyond our influence. This does not mean we are solely subject to their whims. However, it does mean that there are a fair amount of experiences — internal and external — that are beyond our control. We can unpack the paradox of fate and free will another time. For now, let us accept that we have agency to a certain degree and that our goal is to take full advantage of it.

Thus, when it comes to the Realms, our primary job is to regularly attend to each one in the same way we might care for our physical home. Regardless of whether we live in a castle or a cave, we benefit from keeping our dwelling neat and clean, caring for the objects within, clearing the openings, making the atmosphere beautiful according to our temperament, and maybe doing some renovating now and then.

Same holds true for attending to the Realms.

As we do, we learn a lot about them and ourselves. How the Realms relate to one another organically and how they respond to our loving attention and care generates the fuel for Artistry. We learn to listen to them as they guide us towards what will bring forth the most beautiful expression of ourselves in the world.

In this regard, we acknowledge that we are both the Artist and the Art.

As the Artist, we can begin to strategize how to best care for our Realms *and* support their ongoing integration. Once we get the hang of creating a lifestyle that supports Artistry, whenever we feel stuck in our lives, we can readily move through the challenge. Difficult impasses are often due to our attention becoming fixed in one Realm. To get flowing again, we always have two other Realms to turn to for rest, guidance, or inspiration. We never have to be stuck for long.

For example ...

Imagine being faced with an important decision around the diagnosis of a life-threatening illness. You're being asked to decide which avenue of healing to take. In your external reality, doctors, family, friends, scholars, shamans, and experts of all sorts are offering their opinions on what path you should take. You feel overwhelmed and confused.

In addition, you're subject to the activation of all your internal selves in response to the diagnosis. It's likely you're feeling a lot: fear, anxiety, doubt, avoidance, denial, and — if you've already been doing some work in the Realm of the Self — perhaps some wonder, curiosity, acceptance, and courage.

Your thoughts and emotions are likely to be swinging back and forth between optimism and dread. You might feel yourself going crazy trying to sort it all out so you can decide what to do.

Now imagine shifting your attention into the Realm of the Witness.

From here, the Selves are still expressing their thoughts and feelings on the matter, but *you* are not identifying as any one of them, nor are you collapsing into taking action on any one of their preferences. Instead, you're breathing. Simply breathing. Feeling the breath breathing you.

You're allowing your nervous system to settle because you know that fear, anxiety, denial, and avoidance are legitimate feelings, but they do not constitute the foundation from which you need to make your decisions.

Soon you're able to Witness the people around you as well — without getting caught into taking on their points of view. As the experts and do-gooders and family members continue to offer their advice, you're able to allow their views to wash over you without any need to accept or refuse their input.

You continue to breathe and observe. When you're ready, from this calm center, you engage one-on-one with each Self to explore their thoughts and feelings — fully accepting and legitimizing their points of view.

Without worrying about how your decision will come, you fully trust that it will.

Next, you turn your attention towards Source. There you give yourself over to your essence and surrender to this living presence in you and around you. You might choose to expand into becoming pure energy, light, love, or emptiness — however you experience this aliveness. You might invoke the mystery to embrace you, allowing you to release feeling burdened by your human experience. Resting into or merging with Source reminds you that you are and always will be perfectly safe. Even in death.

You stand — if even for a nanosecond — in the truth that you are the embodiment of the paradox of Source and Self and, therefore, that you can't mess anything up. Ever. You experience loving yourself unconditionally and accepting yourself as you are — no matter which road you take with regard to your diagnosis, and no matter the outcome of the path you choose.

You're certain you cannot make a wrong decision.

Now imagine your time in Source taking the shape of a prayer or a meditation, applying whichever technique or ritual that works for you to commune with Source. With your entire being, you sit with Source, opening to receive. You ask for guidance on which direction to take in response to the diagnosis because you know a decision must be made. While no longer worrying about there being an objectively correct choice, you know there is one decision that is right for you. You have faith in the intuitive knowing that eventually comes.

Your decision is clear.

From here, you apply this decision into the Artistry of your life, which now includes your illness, the diagnosis, and your relationship to the diagnosis. As you engage your next steps, you continue to make room for all the people in your life and your own Selves to feel and express their feelings without allowing them on their own accord to change your mind. You include them in every step of your health journey, knowing that there may be course corrections along the way, as diagnoses often have unpredictable trajectories.

Because you have an embodied understanding and experience that each of the three Realms must participate in the choreography of every aspect of your life, you remain at ease with the unfolding. Soon, no matter how difficult life circumstances become, you are meaningfully engaged in the living of them.

Every human faces difficult times not of their choosing and everyone must meet their inevitable death in whatever way it shows up. Nobody is in full control of their destiny, and yet, it appears as if we may have some agency in how we respond to our life circumstances.

Therefore ...

This same process — incorporating the three Realms into real-time decision making — is applied equally to the more mundane choices we must make each day. After all, sometimes even the little decisions can paralyze even the most enlightened amongst us.

Imagine yourself going to a restaurant with a friend at their suggestion. You're excited to spend time with this friend but, when you open the menu, you find yourself frozen around what to order. Recently you've decided to eat more healthily and the menu is filled with all of the unhealthy food you're trying to stop eating.

Imagine noticing your anxiety and stopping for a moment to step back, to Witness, and to breathe. Maybe you ask your friend for a minute of silence, or you head to the bathroom to take one. You make a quick inventory of the Selves who have opinions about the matter.

It's likely that there will be a Self who is ecstatic with the menu and can't wait for you to order — feeling deeply deprived by this new healthy diet idea. Another might come forward with strong criticism and judgment around you even considering breaking the new routine.

Imagine staying with the breath as you turn towards Source. You feel a wave of acceptance coming towards you. You remember that you can't get this wrong. You are loved. You lean in and listen for guidance around the best choice for you right now, and you accept your intuitive hit.

You order — all the while accepting that there will be Selves happy with your decision and Selves who will be angry and annoyed. Imagine allowing them to be as they are in the background of your awareness as you enjoy time with your friend and every bite of your food — no matter what you end up ordering. After all, the next meal will bring another opportunity to choose again.

These examples provide a peek into how Artistry will manifest in real time. You will engage with the three Realms as they integrate and coordinate so that your actions will have integrity — and the gauge of that integrity will be solely in your hands.

A question often arises at this point: Who is the "you" that is doing the Artistry? Is it a Self? Is it the Witness? Is it Source?

The answer: It *feels* like a Self. However, it is a Self unlike all the others.

As you become more conscious of the Realms, you will begin to experience that the one who makes decisions resides in the intersection of all three Realms. This Artist has a very different presence than any of the other Selves. This one lives in your body in a different way. It speaks to you differently. Why? Because it is located in all three Realms simultaneously, whereas all the other Selves live their lives solely in the Realm of the Self.

The Artist Self is a present-moment Self. This one is not bound by past stories or desires of the future. These belong to the rest of the Selves, who are confined to your inner psyche in the Realm of the Self. The Artist's sole purpose is to coordinate the Artistry in precisely the ways we are discussing. It cares for the Selves, embodies the Witness awareness, and interprets guidance from Source. You might choose to call this Artist the authentic-self, the higher-self, or the soul.

However, I invite caution in the naming of this one.

I do not experience the Artist as more or less authentic than any of the other Selves. It is merely different. Thus I personally choose to not use the term authentic-self. I have a similar response to the title higher-self. To presume that this Self is higher than or superior to the other Selves is to begin to dismiss, exile, or shame other Selves. This is dangerous when it comes to the integrity of our selfhood.

As for the term soul, I find this word to be complicated. It carries a variety of often contrary definitions and mythologies around its nature. I prefer to simply lay it down with due respect.

Instead of agreeing on a title, I suggest we opt for engaging in a conversation that explores and explicates our individual experiences of this subtle inner experience. Who knows, maybe what you mean by soul *is* what I mean by Artist.

Regardless ...

For the purpose of accessing the agency of the Artist and the process we are pointing towards here in Selfistry, I suggest you view the Artist as the place in the center where all three Realms overlap, as illustrated in a Venn diagram.

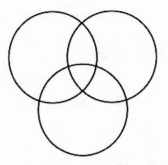

In addition to exploring and deepening in each Realm as we have out-lined in the three prior sections of this book, the other recommended way to become more skillful at your Artistry is to engage in integration practices. The following integration practices will continue to expand your relationship with each Realm individually while strengthening your capacity to move from the integrated center of the Artist — so that you are always making good decisions nimbly on the fly and in the flow of life.

In Selfistry, the integration practices are called Toggling and Still Being Moved. Toggling will bring more precision to the overlap between any two and among all three Realms. Still Being Moved will help you get bet-ter at integrating the Realms by engaging your body in the process.

Toggling

In Toggling, we practice moving our attention deeply into each Realm and then back and forth among them within a single practice session.

Two of the techniques used for this exercise are already familiar to you from the Realms. They are the Sit Down and Shut Up Meditation presented in the Realm of the Witness, and the House Visualization presented in the Realm of the Self. Now we will simply expand these practices from focus in any one particular Realm to include toggling among all three Realms.

The Sit Down and Shut Up Meditation is one of my favorite ways to practice Toggling. Begin by sitting in stillness and silence, bringing your attention onto your breath and finding your way to your inner Witness. As you observe your thoughts, feelings, and sensations receding into the background of your awareness, begin to intentionally pull them into the foreground. As you do, invite the Witness to recede into the background as you become busy thinking, feeling, or sensing. Then pivot your attention back to the Witness. Once there, find your way to placing your attention into the vastness of Source. Maybe at the end of your next exhale, find yourself merging into Source. Once there, rather than staying awhile, pull your attention back into the Witness or the Self.

Continue at your own pace, changing Realms as you are moved. A practice session can last five minutes or an hour. You decide. Just remember, discipline is your friend, and repetition helps us embody what we are learning.

Simply put, Toggling is where you move through the Realms interiorly in no particular order and for no set period of time. In this way, your sitting meditation practice matures. You begin to stretch your capacity to place your attention in one Realm while remaining aware of the other two present in the background. In this way you never lose awareness of any Realm, making it easier to access any one of them at any time.

The question is always the same: Where is my attention?

We learned the House Visualization for the purpose of increasing self-knowledge in the Realm of the Self. I suggested you use this technique primarily to identify Selves, with an exploration of the Witness and Source presented as add-on options.

Now, as a Toggling practice, you will intentionally and actively visit all three Realms equally as you unsystematically move through the entire house. Whereas previously your intention was primarily to meet your Selves, now the goal is to include the other two Realms as important destinations in their own right, and then to experience the impact of organically moving from one to another.

Here is one variation that might help you embody the Artist when engaging the House Visualization as an integration practice.

When it's time to exit the house, imagine the house morphing into a giant vehicle. Set yourself into the driver's seat and take hold of the wheel. Now imagine driving back into your regular life. As you do, notice that all your Selves are with you but that none of them is driving the bus. You, the Artist, are driving. When the Selves try to take over the wheel, you have ways of staying in the driver's seat. You can put the brakes on and stop the bus. You can talk to the Selves who are being disruptive — explore their needs, making sure you address them with compassion and kindness. Or you can pull the vehicle over to the side of the road to take a time out and sit as the Witness or lean into Source for inspiration.

When you are ready, begin to drive again. Don't worry about spending time pulled over and regrouping. There's no rush to get anywhere. There is no need to get your vehicle to some imagined destination where you might finally win a prize or live happily ever after. Truly, there is no place to get to other than right here.

Still Being Moved

Still Being Moved is Selfistry's signature somatic practice. Where Ramana Maharshi taught self-inquiry through the mind, the Still Being Moved practice engages self-inquiry through the body.

This practice is remarkably helpful for Artistry, as mind and body are both crucial to the healthy development of the Artist.

In this somatic practice, you move your body through the Realms. Suggested positions for the body are to take a still posture in the Realm of Source, to stand or sit in loving presence as you inhabit the Realm of the Witness, and to freely move your whole body in the Realm of the Self.

Ideally, for Selfistry events, we use a large clean open space with a great dance floor — nice for the joints — equipped with an excellent sound system ... though music is not essential. We assign areas in the room to each Realm.

In one corner or at one end of the room, we designate a space for the Realm of Source. There we might place cushions or chairs for sitting still and being quiet. You might choose to adorn this area with objects or images that personally orient you to Source.

We designate the periphery of the room as the Realm of the Witness. We keep this area clear of obstructions and make sure there is a view of the entire room.

The center of the room, with the most space for movement, we relegate to the Realm of the Self. You might choose to include support items such as mats, exercise balls, pillows, or blankets in this area to foster your ease of movement and somatic exploration.

When employing sound as part of the experience, the facilitator comes prepared with a music playlist, intentionally curated to include sounds that facilitate a journey both inward and outward, contemplative and expressive, nourishing and activating.

The practice starts with participants sitting in a circle and sharing their intentions for the practice on that day. Once the playlist starts, the participants begin to move their bodies throughout the Realms to explore, listen, and discover.

Using the body to Toggle through the Realms is the magic of Still Being Moved. It plays a significant role in the integration and harmonization of the Realms into our whole being. Plus it's fun.

While the practice of Still Being Moved is my unique creation, born out of my personal attempts to integrate Source and Self in my own being, I would be remiss if I did not note the three somatic lineages that I've learned from and practiced in — and which informed the creation of Still Being Moved.

Nia, Five Rhythms, and *Soul Motion* were each influential in liberating my body, mind, and emotions to express more freely. They were also helpful in teaching me to craft playlists that include intentional arcs and depth, incorporate global music, and attend to the impact of sound and silence on the nervous system.

In many modern techniques of self-development and spiritual growth, body practices are employed. In addition to the three schools mentioned above, there are many others such as Hatha Yoga, Tai Chi, and even weight training. Modern science and ancient teachings speak clearly about the relationship between body and mind. Therefore, Still Being Moved is an essential component of Selfistry, advocating for the full embodiment of the practitioner, recognizing the unarguable importance of a healthy relationship between body and mind.

Still Being Moved got its name as a direct reflection of the Realms and how the body might ideally explore itself in these Realms.

Stillness is the body's ideal architecture when somatically exploring Source. The physiological pause, along with a vertical orientation of the spine, is conducive to a sensed apprehension of the mystery and possibly an experience of first-person communion.

Being grounded and open is the ideal somatic temperament while observing from the Realm of the Witness — establishing a regulated nervous system from which to watch. In this practice, whether you are seated or standing, your gaze is into the whole room and originates from your entire body.

Finally, movement is the invitation for the body in the Realm of the Self — even if those movements are micro or so slow as to hardly be detectable. By taking your body into new and unfamiliar shapes, you gain access to your Selves in a way not often accessible through therapy, journaling, or visualizations. In addition, body movements impact the neural pathways and encourage the neuroplasticity of the brain.

Done in community, Still Being Moved provides support and inspiration. Practicing in groups invokes the power of being with others, replicating the healing somatic experience of allowing our bodies to entrain and regulate with one another in a safe and playful environment.

. . .

In conclusion ...

The two Toggling practices — the Sit Down and Shut Up Meditation and the House Visualization, along with the Still Being Moved somatic practice, will train your mind and body to automatically Toggle in real life, helping guide you to make decisions and take action with integrity.

Over time, you will notice more clarity and confidence in everything you do. You may experience positive shifts in your relationships and work, how you treat yourself and others, and what you choose to put your time and energy towards.

As you make your way through each day, you will readily engage the Witness when you feel the need to pause, take a breath, wonder, and assess. From the Witness Realm, you will bring love and unconditional acceptance into each encounter.

As you navigate tough decisions, you will gracefully include all of your many Selves in your considerations, choosing appropriate and creative opportunities at every turn. You will find yourself no longer bound by the conditioned habits and beliefs you took on growing up, and more in touch with your innate interests and talents. In this way you will engage in meaningful work and fulfilling relationships.

Upon clearing out your learned behaviors and conditioned beliefs regarding spirituality, you will have room for Source to be a living force in your life. As a result, you will be able to access intuition, insight, and inspiration with ease.

When you feel stuck, simply stand back and assess in which Realm you feel the stuckness. Are you suppressing or obsessing over a Self? Are you resisting or hiding out in Source? Or maybe you are paralyzed in the Witness and afraid to take action.

Once you've identified the Realm in which the stuckness is originating, move your attention to one of the other two Realms. Thus begins your Toggling, soon the integration, and then the settling back into your center as the Artist. All that's needed is enough awareness to see and admit that you're stuck.

If you can't tell which Realm you're stuck in or if you feel terribly over-whelmed or confused, consider inviting a trusted friend to offer their observations.

Remember, stuckness is not an indication that you're doing something wrong. We all get stuck. This is natural to our human experience. Our Artistry begins to flow again when we notice, identify, and then engage the stuckness in a way that encourages it to move and change. We grow from being stuck. Flow is not static. It is dynamic. It includes roadblocks as well as open roads.

Activating, integrating, and harmonizing the three Realms is the way to become the Artist of your life.

Remember ...

The depth work in each Realm will serve the Artistry and the Artistry will feed the depth. You can use any adjunct techniques you wish in order to explore each Realm or to facilitate their interplay. In fact, I encourage you to use any and all of the tools in your self-growth toolbox. Simply knowing how to employ them for Artistry will change your life. And it is in the emergence of this life where I believe the whole world will be touched.

And here's how.

When we take the time to look at ourselves and our lives in the way Selfistry speaks of, we create the conditions to see others in a new way as well. Our Witness capacity brings compassion and understanding for the billions of other individuals on this planet and the ways they uniquely express themselves. We can pause our instinct to judge, hate, or do harm to them. With a clear and genuine relationship to Source, we no longer need to hold any religion or belief system above another. Perhaps also, we can begin to create mutual understanding with others as we learn about their way of orienting to this Realm. When we understand that there truly is only one Source, we will have found the way to refrain from harming ourselves, one another, or the planet.

It's true that, as a species, we seem to be a long way from having this kind of understanding of ourselves and one another, but it is possible, and there is a way. The question is whether we will choose to seek it, find it, and practice it.

THESE TIMES

The way of self-renovation.

As I put the final touches on this manuscript, my stepson Gabe and his wife Michelle are in the process of renovating a 100-year-old home in Berkeley. Built in 1920 and designed by architect Julia Morgan, the house is magnificent — plenty of square footage, spacious rooms with high ceilings, and a fabulous yard with dynamite views of the bay. Concrete walls keep the structure earthquake solid and there's more than enough room to house and grow a family of five. So why renovate?

Though the house has many important elements of a suitable home by most standards, it isn't everything Gabe and his family need in order to thrive.

One could argue that the house is fine as it is and, given the cost of renovating, implore them to live with it — to accommodate themselves to the space. It's good enough, after all. In fact, my husband and I lived perfectly well in that house for nearly three years before the demolition for the renovation started.

But during those years, the fireplaces no longer functioned well and were a hazard, the windows leaked air and wasted energy, the attic was dark and the space not utilized well, and the kitchen was tiny, cold, and utilitarian — built for a servant, not for someone like Michelle who loves to cook with her friends and family around her as she does.

The times have changed since that house was built and the needs of individuals, families, and communities are different from what they were 100 years ago. This is a very important consideration. The essential components of Gabe's and Michelle's house are being kept because they still work — along with many of the elements that simply make it beautiful. But the recognition of their needs and their keen discernments on what might be beneficial to the entire family, neighborhood, and community helped them identify where it makes sense to change, upgrade, or recycle.

Similarly, when it comes to what's no longer working or beneficial in our lives, there's a case to be made for the renovation of ourselves. We do not have to tear ourselves down and start from scratch. After all, Gabe and Michelle are not demolishing the entire house. They are preserving the essential and timeless components of their home. Similarly, we might do well by using our discernment to keep what is essential and beautiful within us, as we upgrade the rest to suit what is needed for these times.

As you now know, in Selfistry personal renovation is considered an Art. By taking an inventory of our beliefs and behaviors, assessing the foundation of our worldview, and overhauling our capacity to dispassionately self-reflect, we determine which elements within ourselves no longer serve not only our own personal fulfillment, but the legitimate needs of others as well.

Just as Gabe and Michelle are considering the immediate future of their young family, they are also considering the lives that will outlive them. In deciding it is better to invest in upgrading now rather than leaving things the way they are, they are considering a broad and complex interplay of influences — seen and unseen — in a web that both includes them and transcends them.

Similarly, it makes perfect sense that, in order to engage the present challenges and future opportunities we face as individuals and as a species, we would be wise to consider the value of renovating ourselves today.

Life as we have known it is unraveling and reshaping at an unpredictable pace and the future is perfectly uncertain. Everywhere people are wondering what's happening or what they should do. Everywhere experts are claiming they know what's happening and what we should do. However, the truth is, nobody knows for sure what's happening or what we should do.

One thing we might all agree upon is that finding a way to become the kind of person who can remain calm in the midst of crisis, present in the face of chaos, and capable of remaining steady in any circumstance is probably not a bad idea.

This reminds me of some good advice I received a few years ago from a Native American Grandmother, Agnes Emma Baker Pilgrim, from the Takelma tribe in Southern Oregon. She said that the river of life would be getting wild and fast in our lifetime. She foreshadowed that the impulse might be to grab onto old roots sticking out at the shoreline in order to stop the ride or at least take a break.

"But don't do it," Grandmother warned. "Better to push off from shore than seek it. Get right in the middle of the current. Surface to take a breath, and then see who else is there with you. Bind together and then trust the river. It knows where it's going."

She was right. Life is wild and getting wilder.

Though it can feel terrifying to trust in a strong, wild, and unpredictable current, I suspect Grandmother Aggie's counsel is sensible. Rather than grasp for an elusive stability or try to predict or control the future, I suspect we are well advised to strengthen and reboot ourselves and thus our ability to survive in wild waters so that we may relax into the current without drowning. I say this not because stability or control are bad things to strive for. Rather, they do not appear to be readily available for us collectively right now. If we tell the truth, there are no roots sticking out at the shoreline that can hold us.

ONE LAST STORY

A few years ago at a book reading of my memoir, a young woman in the audience asked me a question.

"After all you have done and been through, what would you say is the meaning of life?"

When I heard the question, my first instinct was to not answer it — to tell her that she needed to find the answer for herself. I wanted her to understand that me telling her what the meaning is from my perspective wouldn't help her, even if it were the truth for her, too. I knew she needed to know what the meaning is *for herself* in order to really live it.

But she was so earnest as she leaned forward from the edge of her chair — her gaze upon me piercing.

How could I let her down?

So I caved.

"The meaning of life is to not miss it — to simply live it," I said.

I wanted to add ...

The meaning of life is *not* to find your purpose, help people, change the world, fix what's broken, earn a seat in heaven, clean your sins from past lives, reach your potential, have fun, love everybody, or even self-reflect and renovate.

Though any or all of the above might happen in any given life, I'm fairly certain that the whole point really is to simply experience the gift of being alive in this moment, and then to meet what life serves up.

Granted, there's a bit of effort and consideration that needs to happen in order to orient this way. Plus, what life is serving up in these times seems especially intense. But truly, the details of life are, you could say, secondary to how we show up for what is here. Without diminishing the significance or impact of any individual life, the point is to not be attached to it looking any particular way.

"That's it?" the young woman practically squealed with disappointment. "Really, after all those years meditating, you're telling me the point of life is just *to live?*"

"Yep," is all I could muster.

At that moment I wanted to invite her to come home with me or at least meet for coffee, because I knew there needed to be more explanation about what I just said — what it means and looks like and how to do it.

I hadn't yet created Selfistry when we met. But I realize now that this is what Selfistry is. Selfistry is the rest of the answer to her question. It is an explanation and elaboration on why the imperative to *just live* makes perfect sense — and why it is best not to delay while you seek some illusory higher purpose — for you might miss this moment and your unique place in it. It is also a road map to help you finally get to right here.

"Easier said than done," the young woman said with defeat.

"I know," I said. "I get it."

I really do.

If I could speak to her now, I would add, "Maybe Selfistry can help make it easier done than said."

GRATITUDE

No creative endeavor is ever born in isolation. Seen and unseen forces always conspire.

Firstly, I want to thank Source for incessantly filling me with the inspiration and invitation to create. The boundless force of love and support I experience from Source is infinite.

There are those who've been close all through this project ... there for the gestation, the work, the re-work, the edits, the revisions, the frustrations, the questioning, the tearing down, and the building up — the pure ecstasy and agony of the writing process.

Adell Shay entered my life at the time when the manuscript was in its early phase. Her devotion to truth and respect for the perspectives I was articulating aroused in her a desire to help. So I invited her to be my writing buddy, where she would support me in whatever ways I needed or didn't even know I needed. Her depth of understanding of the material helped me sort out how to talk about notions that often felt inaccessible to the average person, and her loving heart helped me stay encouraged during times when I felt lost or stuck. Together we built a deep and enduring friendship around a shared mission to make spiritual teachings more accessible and understandable.

Kathryn Thomas is my copy editor. She swoops in and does the polishing of pretty much everything I write for public consumption. She's truly masterful. But more than solely a superstar copy editor, she is a beloved friend and soul sister. Her fierce passion for the embodied elements of Selfistry has brought her to lead the Still Being Moved practice for practitioners all over the world.

Then there's Alyssa.

Alyssa Morin is to me like a daughter, sister, and grandmother all wrapped up into one magnificent bundle of a woman. Her depth of understanding in matters subtle and complex, along with her capacity to make art with words, has contributed not only to this manuscript but to all aspects of Selfistry.

And, of course, there's my beloved husband, Steve Marshank. He's been here for every step of Selfistry's emergence into the world and each crossed-t and dotted-i in this book. He deserves high praise for his patience and unyielding support of me and my work. Add this to how he shows up for our family and the world, and I often wonder how he manages to be so consistently present for so much. I'm honestly not sure how I came to be worthy of the blessing of such a partner in life, but to whomever or whatever is in charge of these things I'm eternally grateful.

Somewhere along the way it became time to get feedback from readers — people who were to varying degrees familiar with me and with Selfistry. The folks who responded to my outreach for volunteers offered invaluable feedback on content and presentation. They were a stellar group. In addition to the takeaways that got incorporated into the manuscript's revision, it was a beautiful process in itself to share the work while it was in process — to let my efforts to communicate something so dear to me land in the minds and hearts of others, and then to open to their reflections. I experienced this stage of the journey as deeply nourishing of my relationship with my audience.

Thank you Nova Jax Dieter, Kim Burns, Beth Levin, Gracia Larson, Erin Anzelmo, Nina Larson, Kari King, Julie Dickens, Howie Schechter, Trisha Wallace, Karen Kleid, and Michael Kreigsman.

A special thank you to my beloved stepdaughter Arianna Marshank, who also stepped in at this stage and offered her insights and reflections. Her astute comments regarding generational and social nuances that I was unaware of was invaluable. But more, her intelligent questions and reflections brought a perspective to the work that was genuinely unique and greatly appreciated. She is a powerful and passionate young woman whom I continue to learn from and grow with.

Once I integrated the feedback from the group of readers and had a revised version of the manuscript in hand, it was time to engage in a round with a professional content editor.

This is a stunning story.

As I was searching for the right person, I connected with Corinne Dixon, a woman who'd attended a course I taught a few years prior. I knew she had editing experience and asked her if she would be interested in editing my manuscript. She was delighted, as she was just launching her own book-editing business called *Abookadabra - manuscript enchantment.* "How serendipitous," we both thought.

Corinne's day job at the time was with the First Nation people in British Columbia. She was planning a slow transition to the launch of her business as she closed in on her 60th birthday. We had a series of meetings to arrange our contract and plan our course of action. I then sent her the first section of the manuscript. She emailed me to say she received it, loved it, and was going to send me her specific suggestions within a week. And then she died.

Before I learned of her sudden death, I knew that Corinne was managing some health challenges, which she had mentioned, but in no way did I get the impression that she was close to dying. I now know that neither did she.

After not receiving the promised suggestions and reaching out to her with no response — and having had no connection with her friends or family — I went to her Facebook page. There was the news. She had died suddenly of what seemed to be a heart attack.

I was shocked and devastated.

The abruptness of her death on the heels of our rekindled friendship and partnership on this project left me breathless and in tears. The grief that poured through me felt deep and raw and tethered to so much other grief ... for the planet and humanity and my own mortality. There was no possible completion for me with dear Corinne in this world, so I took to my meditation cushion and found my way to speaking with her from within. She encouraged me to carry on, that what she had read was good, that another editor would show up, and not to worry.

I worried nonetheless.

How could I find another such perfect match? Corinne's understanding of the content, as well as her approach to writing, were so resonant. I felt wholly adrift.

Then, out of the blue, Edith reached out.

Edith Friesen was my editor and writing coach on my first book. In retrospect it seems obvious that she would be the one. But I suspect that, at the time, I had imagined her not being available, as she was working on her own writing project. And yet, there she was that day, simply reaching out as a friend, checking in to say hello. When I told her about

Corinne, she did not hesitate. She offered to edit the manuscript and would not accept no for an answer.

I burst into tears. And then I said yes.

Edith's editing felt like bringing in a fine-tooth comb made of gold. She captured all the subtle inconsistencies and areas needing further explanation — sometimes addressable by the changing of one word. Masterfully and lovingly, she helped me bring the manuscript one step closer to publication.

Some people think I am a perfectionist. I can own that perception — though I prefer to say I have an appreciation for excellence and recognize the unattainability of perfection. And yet ... I admit. I fall prey.

So after Edith had done her magic and I had made my changes, I felt the call for one more copy editor to read through the manuscript — in addition to Kathryn. Enter my dear friend Deborah-Miriam Leff and her keen eye for detail.

Then covid hit.

I felt the context of the project change and saw the importance of addressing the crisis. The need to incorporate the pandemic into the tone — if not the content — of the book became evident. So I dove in again for another revision, working more deeply with the framing of why Selfistry is so relevant to these times.

Most recently, I received final reader feedback from Jolene Monheim and Cate Verdin, each offering explicit and powerful pushback to help bring the project to clarity and completion.

At some point a writer knows when to lay down the pen and call the work finished. Though I had hoped the project would take less time, I know better than to force or rush art. Like the Artistry of our lives, there is a cadence and a rhythm that informs the Art beyond the control of the Artist.

Therefore I would be remiss if I did not take a moment to thank all the Selves inside of me. I'm grateful for the creative tension generated through their resistance and the consequent creativity that always ensues. I appreciate their patience with one another, their acceptance of the fearful ones, their holding of the ones whose survival felt dependent on getting it right, alongside the ones who did everything in their power to get us to throw the whole damn book away and do something else with our life.

Clearly, the creation of this book is an example *and* product of the Artistry called Selfistry.

Thus ...

More than five years after one of my Selves sat down to write the first draft, we all agree to now lay down our pens.

ABOUT THE AUTHOR

It was 1988 when one of my favorite students asked me the question that would set the trajectory of my life.

Just having completed course work for my master's degree in History and Philosophy of Education, I was teaching full time while finishing my thesis exploring the relevance of Rudolph Steiner's pedagogy to the evolution of public education in the US. I was twenty-five years old.

When I took the fifth-grade job, I was already implementing principles of alternative education, including individualized learning styles, an integrative curriculum that evoked discovery rather than consumption of data, and weekly class meetings to talk about our feelings. But when Daniel asked me his question, I was unprepared for the way it touched me.

It was during one of our Friday circles. We were discussing a quarrel that had ignited between two of the kids earlier in the week on the playground. While we were untangling some lingering tension, Daniel looked at me squarely and asked, "What would God say?"

That was it.

The question that changed everything.

What would God say?

I had no idea what God would say, or what God even was. I was teaching in a Jewish private school so I knew the party line. But my love for Daniel would not allow me to give him a rote answer or in any way dismiss the gravity of his question.

Acknowledging that I did not know, I invited him to wonder along with me what God might say. While this tactic felt right in that moment, it was insufficient for my aching heart. Pondering the exchange that evening while soaking in a hot bath, I resolved that I would never again put myself in the position of being unable to address such an essential inquiry from within the depth of my own knowledge and experience.

And so began my quest in earnest for the answer to Daniel's question — which, of course, was actually mine.

My journey of discovery was rich with intensity and controversy, extreme in its execution but fruitful in its yield. I share the details in my memoir, Redefining Being Self-ish: My Journey from Escort to Monk to Grandmother.

Selfistry is the lovechild born from my passion for education and my longing for God or Truth. Its pedagogy includes my embodied knowledge from a decade in retreat, my formal academic training, and my advanced learning in Integral Theory, Psychotherapy, Human Development, and Organizational Leadership.

During the publication of this manuscript, I'm living with my husband in the hills of Oakland, California — close to our three beloved granddaughters. However, at the precise moment you're reading this, I could be anywhere. Selfistry has a presence in many regions of the planet, including the UK, the Netherlands, Germany, Poland, Mexico, Canada, and Australia. Therefore, as the pandemic stabilizes and political unrest calms, you might find me in any of these places, as one of my selves is a happy digital nomad.

Selfistry is a body of work. But more, it is a living system. It changes and grows just like you and me. Reach out to me via sarah@selfistry.com to learn more about what's happening right now and to explore how we might join together in service to the global reboot that is underway. I'd love to hear from you.